WeightWatchers®

Delicious recipes for everyone

Perfect Pasta

D0307561

First published in Great Britain by Simon & Schuster UK Ltd, 2014
A CBS Company

Copyright © 2014, Weight Watchers International, Inc.
Simon & Schuster Illustrated Books, Simon & Schuster UK Ltd,
First Floor, 222 Gray's Inn Road, London WC1X 8HB

www.simonandschuster.co.uk

Simon & Schuster Australia, Sydney
Simon & Schuster India, New Delhi

Weight Watchers, **ProPoints** and the **ProPoints** icon are the registered trademarks
of Weight Watchers International Inc. and are used under license by Weight Watchers
(UK) Ltd.

Weight Watchers Publications: Lucy Clements, Imogen Prescott, Nina McKerlie.

Recipes written by: Sue Ashworth, Sue Beveridge, Sara Buenfeld,
Tamsin Burnett-Hall, Cas Clarke, Siân Davies, Roz Denny, Nicola Graimes,
Becky Johnson, Kim Morphew, Joy Skipper, Penny Stephens and Wendy Veale
as well as Weight Watchers Leaders and Members.

Photography by: Iain Bagwell, Steve Baxter, Will Heap, Steve Lee, Lis Parsons,
Juliet Piddington and William Shaw.
Project editor: Sharon Amos.
Design and typesetting: Geoff Fennell.
Proofreading: Jane Bamforth.

Printed and bound in China.

A CIP catalogue record for this book is available from the British Library

ISBN 978-1-47113-164-6

10 9 8 7 6 5 4 3 2 1

Pictured on the title page: Courgette and cherry tomato pasta p88.
Pictured on the Introduction: Lasagne p38, Linguine with broad beans and rocket p100,
Creamy sausage and mustard pasta p92.

WeightWatchers®

Delicious recipes for everyone

Perfect Pasta

SIMON &
SCHUSTER
ILLUSTRATED

London · New York · Sydney · Toronto · New Delhi

A CBS COMPANY

If you would like to find out more about Weight Watchers and the **ProPoints** Plan, please visit: www.weightwatchers.co.uk

Ⓥ This symbol denotes a vegetarian recipe and assumes that, where relevant, free range eggs, vegetarian cheese, vegetarian virtually fat free fromage frais, vegetarian low fat crème fraîche and vegetarian low fat yogurts are used. Virtually fat free fromage frais, low fat crème fraîche and low fat yogurts may contain traces of gelatine so they are not always vegetarian. Please check the labels.

❅ This symbol denotes a dish that can be frozen. Unless otherwise stated, you can freeze the finished dish for up to 3 months. Defrost thoroughly and reheat until the dish is piping hot throughout.

Recipe notes

Egg size: Medium, unless otherwise stated.

Raw eggs: Only the freshest eggs should be used. Pregnant women, the elderly and children should avoid recipes with eggs that are not fully cooked or raw.

All fruits and vegetables: Medium, unless otherwise stated.

Stock: Stock cubes are used in recipes, unless otherwise stated. These should be prepared according to packet instructions.

Timings: These are approximate and meant to be guidelines.

Microwaves: Timings and temperatures are for a standard 800 W microwave. If necessary, adjust your own microwave.

Low fat spread: Where a recipe states to use a low fat spread, a light spread with a fat content of no less than 38% should be used.

Low fat soft cheese: Where low fat soft cheese is specified in a recipe, this refers to soft cheese with a fat content of less than 5%.

ProPoints values: Should you require the **ProPoints** values for any of the recipes within this book, you can call Customer Services on 0845 345 1500 and we will provide you with the relevant information on a recipe-by-recipe basis. Please allow 28 days for us to provide you with this information.

Contents

Introduction

Where would we be without pasta? Every day mums and dads all over the country turn to pasta for a quick and filling way to feed the family. That's why we've included recipes for family favourites such as Lasagne, Spaghetti Bolognese, Pasta Carbonara, and Welsh Leek and Pasta Bake.

But pasta isn't just a quick family filler; you'll also find sophisticated supper dishes for two, such as Smoked Salmon Linguine, and treats for when you're eating alone, such as Crab and Rocket Linguine or Grilled Teriyaki Salmon and Pasta. Then there are hearty soups and dishes for leisurely weekend get togethers – look out for Spinach and Mushroom Cannelloni, Baked Aubergine Pasta or Penne with Lamb Ragù.

And while you're cooking supper, we've suggested simple salad recipes such as Pesto Pasta Salad and Spicy Crab Pasta Salad that you can prepare alongside and pack up ready for tomorrow's lunchbox.

About Weight Watchers

For more than 40 years Weight Watchers has been helping people around the world to lose weight using a long term sustainable approach. Weight Watchers successful weight loss system is based on four tried and trusted principles:

- Eating healthily
- Being more active
- Adjusting behaviour to help weight loss
- Getting support in weekly meetings

Our unique **ProPoints** system empowers you to manage your food plan and make wise recipe choices for a healthier, happier you.

Storing and freezing

Many dishes store well in the fridge, but make sure you use them up within a day or two. Some can also be frozen. However, it is important to make sure you know how to freeze ingredients and dishes safely.

- Wrap any food to be frozen in rigid containers or strong freezer bags. This is important to stop foods contaminating each other or getting freezer burn.
- Label the containers or bags with the contents and date – your freezer should have a star marking that tells you how long you can keep different types of frozen food.
- Never freeze warm food – always let it cool completely first.
- Never freeze food that has already been frozen and defrosted.
- Freeze food in portions, then you can take out as little or as much as you need each time.
- Defrost what you need in the fridge, making sure you put anything that might have juices, such as meat, on a covered plate or in a container.
- Fresh food, such as raw chicken, should be wrapped and frozen as soon as possible.
- Most fruit and vegetables can be frozen by open freezing. Lay them out on a tray, freeze until solid and then pack them into bags.
- Some fresh vegetables, such as peas, broccoli and broad beans can be blanched first by cooking for 2 minutes in boiling water. Drain, refresh under cold water and then freeze once cold.

- Fresh herbs freeze well – seal leaves in bags or, for soft herbs such as basil and parsley, chop finely and add to ice cube trays with water. Drop them into casseroles or soups straight from the freezer.

Some things cannot be frozen. Whole eggs do not freeze well, but yolks and whites can be frozen separately. Vegetables with a high water content, such as salad leaves, celery and cucumber, will not freeze. Fried foods will be soggy if frozen, and sauces such as mayonnaise will separate when thawed and should not be frozen.

Shopping hints and tips

Always buy the best ingredients you can afford. If you are going to cook healthy meals, it is worth investing in some quality ingredients that will really add flavour to your dishes. When buying meat, choose lean cuts of meat or lean mince, and if you are buying prepacked cooked, sliced meat, buy it fresh from the deli counter.

When you're going around the supermarket it's tempting to pick up foods you like and put them in your trolley without thinking about how you will use them. So, a good plan is to decide what dishes you want to cook before you go shopping, check your storecupboard and make a list of what you need. You'll save time by not drifting aimlessly around the supermarket picking up what you fancy.

We've added a checklist here for some common storecupboard ingredients. Make sure you stock up on as many different types of pasta as you'll need. Just add fresh ingredients to your regular shop and you'll be ready to cook *Perfect Pasta*.

Storecupboard checklist

- [ ] basil, dried
- [ ] bay leaves
- [ ] borlotti beans, canned
- [ ] capers in brine
- [ ] chick peas, canned
- [ ] chilli flakes, dried
- [ ] cinnamon, ground
- [ ] cloves
- [ ] cooking spray, calorie controlled
- [ ] coriander seeds
- [ ] cornflour
- [ ] couscous, dried
- [ ] crab meat, canned in brine
- [ ] cumin seeds
- [ ] curry (paste and powder)
- [ ] dill, dried
- [ ] flour, plain
- [ ] French dressing, low fat
- [ ] harissa paste
- [ ] honey, clear
- [ ] jalapeño peppers, in brine
- [ ] kidney beans, canned
- [ ] lasagne sheets, dried
- [ ] mace, ground
- [ ] mayonnaise, extra light
- [ ] mustard (Dijon, French and wholegrain)
- [ ] nutmeg
- [ ] oil (vegetable, olive, sesame)
- [ ] olives in brine, black
- [ ] olives, pimento stuffed
- [ ] oregano, dried
- [ ] paprika (regular and smoked)
- [ ] passata
- [ ] pasta, dried, a selection of types
- [ ] peppercorns
- [ ] peppers, roasted, in a jar
- [ ] pesto
- [ ] pine nut kernels
- [ ] salad cream, light
- [ ] salt
- [ ] sardines, canned in brine
- [ ] sauce flour
- [ ] stock cubes, all types
- [ ] sugar
- [ ] sun-dried tomatoes in oil
- [ ] sweetcorn, canned
- [ ] Tabasco sauce
- [ ] teriyaki marinade
- [ ] tomato ketchup
- [ ] tomato purée
- [ ] tomatoes, canned
- [ ] tuna, canned in brine
- [ ] vinaigrette, fat free
- [ ] vinegar (balsamic and wine)
- [ ] walnut halves
- [ ] wine, red and white
- [ ] Worcestershire sauce

Simply salads

Asparagus pasta salad with blue cheese dressing

Serves 4
267 calories per serving
Takes 15 minutes

175 g (6 oz) dried penne
200 g (7 oz) thin asparagus
spears, chopped roughly
15 g (½ oz) pine nut kernels
50 g (1¾ oz) blue cheese,
crumbled
100 g (3½ oz) low fat natural
yogurt
75 g (2¾ oz) baby spinach
leaves
freshly ground black pepper

Blue cheese makes a rich-tasting dressing without too many calories. A small amount gives a lot of flavour.

1 Bring a large pan of water to the boil and cook the pasta according to the packet instructions, adding the asparagus spears for the last 3 minutes of cooking time.

2 Meanwhile, in a non-stick frying pan, dry fry the pine nut kernels for 1–2 minutes, shaking until golden brown. Set aside.

3 In a mixing bowl, crumble the blue cheese, mash with a fork and gradually mix in the yogurt to make the dressing. Season to taste with freshly ground black pepper.

4 Drain the pasta and asparagus and rinse in cold water. Tip into the mixing bowl and toss with the blue cheese dressing to coat, mixing in the spinach leaves at the same time. Serve scattered with the toasted pine nut kernels.

Pasta and sweet pepper salad

Serves 4
260 calories per serving
Takes 20 minutes

175 g (6 oz) dried pasta
shapes
1 courgette, chopped
1 red pepper, de-seeded and
sliced
1 yellow pepper, de-seeded
and sliced
1 small red onion, thinly sliced
4 spring onions, trimmed and
finely chopped
12 cherry tomatoes, halved
12 stoned black olives
salt and freshly ground black
pepper
a few sprigs of fresh oregano
or parsley, to garnish

For the dressing
1 tablespoon olive oil
1 tablespoon red or white
wine vinegar
1 tablespoon sun-dried tomato
purée
2 tablespoons chopped fresh
oregano or parsley

Lots of crunchy vegetables with pungent black olives and a Mediterranean tomato dressing.

1 Bring a large pan of water to the boil and cook the pasta according to the packet instructions.

2 Meanwhile, cook the courgette in a small amount of boiling water for 3–4 minutes. Drain and refresh under cold running water.

3 To make the dressing, mix together the olive oil, vinegar, sun-dried tomato purée and chopped herbs. Season well.

4 Drain the pasta and tip it into a large serving bowl. Add the dressing and toss well. Add the courgette, peppers, red onion, spring onions, cherry tomatoes and olives, stirring to mix. Serve, garnished with sprigs of fresh oregano or parsley.

Variations… Use tomato purée if you haven't got sun-dried tomato purée. Add more vegetables if you like: try chopped cucumber, tiny cauliflower florets or sliced mushrooms.

Chilli prawn farfalle salad

Serves 4
295 calories per serving
Takes 15 minutes

225 g (8 oz) dried farfalle pasta
150 g (5½ oz) baby corn, halved
1 red chilli, de-seeded and sliced in strips
450 g (1 lb) tiger prawns, cooked and peeled
6 tablespoons fat free vinaigrette

A really quick salad with delicious tiger prawns and a hint of fiery chilli.

1 Bring a large pan of water to the boil, add the pasta and cook according to the packet instructions. Add the baby corn for the last 4 minutes of cooking time. Drain the pasta and corn, and rinse in cold water.

2 Toss all the ingredients together and serve.

Pesto pasta salad

Serves 1
282 calories per serving
Takes 10 minutes

40 g (1½ oz) dried mini pasta
  shapes, e.g. conchigliette
  or farfalline
60 g (2 oz) asparagus spears,
  chopped roughly
60 g (2 oz) broccoli, broken
  into small florets
1 tablespoon pesto
½ red pepper, de-seeded and
  cubed
6 cherry tomatoes, quartered

This pasta salad is quick to make and can easily be prepared alongside your evening meal, ready to take to work the following day.

1 Bring a large pan of water to the boil and add the pasta, asparagus and broccoli and cook according to the instructions on the pasta packet. Rinse in cold water and drain well.

2 Mix the cooked pasta and vegetables with the pesto, red pepper and cherry tomatoes.

Roasted vegetable pasta salad

Serves 4

389 calories per serving

Takes 15 minutes to prepare,
30 minutes to cook +
30 minutes chilling

Ⓥ

1 large butternut squash,
de-seeded and cut into
chunks

2 red onions, cut into wedges

1 red pepper, de-seeded and
cut into chunks

1 yellow pepper, de-seeded
and cut into chunks

calorie controlled cooking
spray

2 teaspoons coriander seeds

1 teaspoon cumin seeds

250 g (9 oz) dried cavatappi
(spiral macaroni)

For the dressing

1 tablespoon fat free dressing

3 tablespoons 0% fat Greek
yogurt

1 tablespoon medium curry
paste

2 tablespoons chopped fresh
parsley

salt and freshly ground black
pepper

*Roasting the vegetables first brings out the sweetness and
concentrates their flavour.*

1 Preheat the oven to Gas Mark 7/220°C/fan oven 200°C.
Place all the vegetables in a large roasting tin, in a single layer.
Spray with the cooking spray.

2 Heat a dry frying pan until hot. Dry fry the coriander and
cumin seeds over a medium heat for 2 minutes until they pop
and their aroma is released, then crush and sprinkle them over
the vegetables. Roast the vegetables for 30 minutes, stirring
occasionally, until tender and lightly charred. Remove from the
oven and leave to cool.

3 Bring a large pan of water to the boil and cook the pasta
according to the packet instructions. Drain and rinse in plenty
of cold water.

4 Mix together the dressing ingredients and pour over the
pasta, stirring in the vegetables. Season to taste, cool and chill
for 30 minutes to allow the flavours to develop.

Egg and avocado pasta salad

Serves 4
337 calories per serving
Takes 20 minutes

3 eggs
200 g (7 oz) dried pasta shells
150 g (5½ oz) mange tout,
halved
1 ripe avocado
2 tablespoons snipped fresh
chives
4 tablespoons fat free salad
dressing
100 g (3½ oz) baby spinach
leaves
freshly ground black pepper

A mixture of 'greens' topped with hard-boiled eggs for a light summer lunch.

1 Place the eggs in a small saucepan, cover with cold water and bring to the boil. Simmer for 6 minutes, then place in cold water to cool. Peel and cut into quarters.

2 Meanwhile, bring a large pan of water to the boil and cook the pasta according to the packet instructions. Add the mange tout for the last 2 minutes of cooking time. Drain and rinse in cold water.

3 While the pasta is cooking, cut the avocado in half and remove the stone. Use a dessertspoon to scoop the avocado flesh from the skin in one piece, then cut it into cubes. Mix the avocado, chives and dressing together in a bowl, then stir in the drained pasta and mange tout, followed by the spinach. Add freshly ground pepper, to taste, and serve topped with the hard-boiled eggs.

Spicy crab pasta salad

This delicious pasta salad with a creamy dressing and spicy salsa is ideal for lunch or to take on a picnic.

Serves 2

293 calories per serving

Takes 20 minutes

For the salsa

4 spring onions, trimmed and sliced finely

2 tomatoes, de-seeded and cubed

1 small red chilli, de-seeded and cubed

finely grated zest and juice of a lime

1 tablespoon roughly chopped fresh coriander leaves

For the pasta

110 g (4 oz) dried fusilli

170 g can crab meat in brine, drained

1 tablespoon light salad cream

3 tablespoons 0% fat Greek yogurt

1 teaspoon paprika

salt and freshly ground black pepper

1 Mix the salsa ingredients together and set aside to allow the flavours to develop.

2 Bring a large pan of water to the boil and cook the pasta according to the packet instructions. Drain and rinse under cold water.

3 Mix the crab, salad cream, yogurt, paprika and seasoning into the pasta. Serve the salsa alongside or mixed in if you prefer.

Tips… Try using crab sticks instead of the canned crab. Shred 8 crab sticks and mix into the pasta with the dressing – they're sold on most supermarket fish counters.

Serve the salad with a handful of rocket if you like.

Tricolore pasta salad

Serves 1
291 calories per serving
Takes 12 minutes

40 g (1½ oz) dried mini pasta shells

60 g (2 oz) broccoli, cut into tiny florets

½ a yellow or orange pepper, de-seeded and cubed

100 g (3½ oz) cherry tomatoes, halved

25 g (1 oz) Edam cheese, cut into small cubes

1 tablespoon shredded fresh basil

1 tablespoon low fat French dressing

Prepare this colourful pasta salad the night before and pack it into a lunchbox, ready to take to work. Or make it for a picnic.

1 Bring a large pan of water to the boil and cook the pasta according to the packet instructions. Add the broccoli to the pan for the final 2 minutes of cooking.

2 Drain the pasta and broccoli and rinse in cold water. Drain again.

3 Mix the pepper, tomatoes, Edam, basil and French dressing together in a bowl. Stir in the pasta and broccoli, then serve.

Spinach pasta salad with roasted red pepper dressing

Serves 4

240 calories per serving

Takes 15 minutes to prepare,
15 minutes to cook

**150 g (5½ oz) dried spinach,
tomato or plain pasta**

**200 g (7 oz) spinach, stems
removed, or baby spinach
leaves**

**100 g (3½ oz) low fat soft
cheese**

**1 tablespoon pine nut kernels,
toasted (optional)**

For the dressing

2 red peppers

1 garlic clove, crushed

**1 tablespoon balsamic vinegar
or apple juice**

1 teaspoon sugar

**salt and freshly ground black
pepper**

*Coloured pasta looks pretty and adds a subtly different
flavour to this salad.*

1 Bring a large pan of water to the boil and cook the pasta
according to the packet instructions. Drain and immediately
toss with the spinach in a large bowl. The heat from the pasta
should just wilt the spinach.

2 Grill the red peppers until they are blackened on all sides,
then place them in a plastic bag and leave until cool enough to
handle. Peel away the charred skin, cut the peppers open and
remove the seeds. Place the flesh in a liquidiser with the other
dressing ingredients and 2 tablespoons of water and process
until smooth. Check the seasoning before pouring over the
spinach and pasta.

3 Crumble the cheese on top of the salad and sprinkle with
the pine nut kernels, if using.

Tip... To toast pine nut kernels, dry fry them in a non-stick
frying pan over a medium heat for 2–3 minutes until golden.
Do not let them burn.

Spiced tuna and pasta salad

Serves 4

140 calories per serving

Takes 15 minutes

125 g (4½ oz) pasta shapes,
  cooked

200 g can tuna steak in brine,
  drained

450 g (1 lb) tomatoes,
  quartered and de-seeded

1 red onion, sliced finely

1 fresh chilli, de-seeded and
  chopped finely or 1 teaspoon
  chilli powder

25 g packet fresh coriander,
  chopped

For the dressing

1 teaspoon ground cumin

2 teaspoons extra virgin
  olive oil

juice of a lemon

1 teaspoon sugar

salt and freshly ground
  black pepper

A simple salad that's bursting with gutsy flavours. It's especially good with wholewheat pasta.

1 Make the dressing by putting the ingredients in a small bowl and whisking briskly with a fork.

2 Put the pasta and the rest of the salad ingredients in a large serving bowl. Add the dressing, toss well to mix, and serve.

Sausage and rocket pasta salad

Serves 2

228 calories per serving

Takes 20 minutes to prepare
+ 10 minutes cooling

2 thick low fat pork sausages
75 g (2¾ oz) dried pasta bows
60 g (2 oz) asparagus tips
**1 red pepper, de-seeded and
cubed into 1 cm (½ inch)
pieces**
25 g (1 oz) rocket leaves

For the dressing

**4 tablespoons 0% fat Greek
yogurt**
**2 teaspoons wholegrain
mustard**

*In this summery salad, the creamy mustard dressing
complements the sausages beautifully and rocket adds
just enough hot peppery flavour.*

1 Preheat the grill to medium and line the grill pan with foil.
Cook the sausages for 7–8 minutes, turning, until golden all
over. Remove from the heat and when cool, slice each one into
five pieces.

2 Meanwhile, bring a large pan of water to the boil and cook
the pasta according to the packet instructions, adding the
asparagus tips for the final 5 minutes of cooking. Drain and
rinse with cold water until cool. Drain again.

3 Mix together the dressing ingredients in a large serving bowl
and toss with the sausage pieces, pasta, asparagus, red pepper
and rocket.

Tip... Make the salad an hour in advance without the
rocket, then cover and chill until required, mixing in the
rocket before serving. This allows the flavours to develop.

Spring vegetable and pasta salad

Serves 4
320 calories per serving
Takes 20 minutes

250 g (9 oz) dried pasta
  ribbons (e.g. tagliatelle or
  fettuccine)
150 g (5½ oz) mange tout
150 g (5½ oz) baby carrots
250 g (9 oz) baby corn
175 g (6 oz) baby leeks
150 g (5½ oz) broccoli,
  chopped into florets

For the dressing
juice and zest of a lemon
2 teaspoons extra virgin olive
  oil
25 g packet fresh basil, torn,
  or fresh coriander, chopped
25 g packet fresh chervil,
  chopped
25 g packet fresh parsley,
  chopped
1 teaspoon clear honey
salt and freshly ground black
  pepper

You can vary the herbs in this fresh zesty salad, depending on what you have to hand.

1 Bring 2 large pans of water to the boil. To one add the pasta and cook according to the packet instructions. Drain and place in a large serving bowl. To the other pan add the vegetables and cook until just done – about 3 minutes. Drain and add to the pasta.

2 In a bowl, mix together all the dressing ingredients and pour over the warm vegetables and pasta. Toss and serve.

Family favourites

Lasagne

Serves 6

250 calories per serving

Takes 40 minutes to prepare,
35 minutes to cook

❄ (for up to 1 month)

calorie controlled cooking
spray

1 small onion, chopped finely

2 unsmoked bacon rashers,
chopped finely

1 garlic clove, crushed

200 g (7 oz) extra lean beef
mince

1 teaspoon dried basil

400 g can chopped tomatoes

2 tablespoons tomato purée

150 ml (5 fl oz) beef stock

200 g (7 oz) virtually fat free
fromage frais

50 ml (2 fl oz) soya milk

50 g (1¾ oz) low fat soft
cheese

freshly grated nutmeg

225 g (8 oz) lasagne sheets

salt and freshly ground black
pepper

The classic Italian dish with a clever low fat white sauce that retains all the traditional flavour.

1 Preheat the oven to Gas Mark 4/180°C/fan oven 160°C. Heat a lidded frying pan sprayed with the cooking spray and cook the onion, bacon and garlic for 5 minutes. Add the beef and brown, stirring constantly.

2 Stir in the basil, chopped tomatoes, tomato purée, beef stock and seasoning. Bring to a simmer. Cover and cook for 15–20 minutes.

3 Mix together the fromage frais, soya milk and soft cheese to make a smooth white sauce. Add the nutmeg and seasoning.

4 Spread about a quarter of the beef sauce over the base of an ovenproof dish. Cover with sheets of lasagne and a few spoonfuls of white sauce. Repeat these layers, finishing with a final layer of white sauce. Bake in the oven for 30–35 minutes until the sauce is bubbling and golden.

Cheesy pasta and ham bake

Serves 4
430 calories per serving
Takes 40 minutes

**200 g (7 oz) dried pasta
shapes**
**4 medium-thick slices lean
ham, weighing approx 150 g
(5½ oz) in total, sliced into
small pieces**
**a small bunch of parsley,
chopped finely**
2 tablespoons low fat spread
2 tablespoons plain flour
600 ml (20 fl oz) skimmed milk
1 tablespoon French mustard
**100 g (3½ oz) low fat soft
cheese**
**50 g (1¾ oz) half fat Cheddar
cheese, grated**
**salt and freshly ground black
pepper**

*A family favourite that is quick and easy to make and will
fill everyone up. Serve with sugar snap peas and grilled
tomatoes.*

1 Bring a large pan of water to the boil and cook the pasta
according to the packet instructions, but drain it when it is still
slightly undercooked. Place it in a large ovenproof dish. Add the
ham and parsley. Preheat the oven to Gas Mark 6/200°C/fan
oven 180°C.

2 Meanwhile make the sauce by melting the low fat spread
in a non-stick saucepan. Add the flour and stir together for a
minute. Then add the milk, a little at a time, and stir vigorously
between each addition, until it is smoothly combined.

3 Add the mustard, soft cheese and seasoning, and stir in.
Pour the sauce over the pasta and toss it all together until
evenly combined. Sprinkle with the grated Cheddar and bake
for 20 minutes, or until golden and bubbling.

Variation… Vegetarians would also enjoy this dish – just
omit the ham.

Prawn and tomato pasta bake

Serves 4

405 calories per serving

Takes 30 minutes to prepare,
25 minutes to cook

calorie controlled cooking
spray

1 medium onion, chopped
finely

2 small red chillies, de-seeded
and chopped finely

2 garlic cloves, chopped finely

2 x 400 g cans chopped
tomatoes

2 teaspoons dried oregano

500 ml (18 fl oz) skimmed milk

4 tablespoons sauce flour

80 g (3 oz) half fat Cheddar
cheese, freshly grated

150 g (5½ oz) dried rigatoni

200 g (7 oz) cooked, peeled
prawns

150 g (5½ oz) cherry
tomatoes, halved

2 tablespoons finely grated
Parmesan cheese

salt and freshly ground black
pepper

Try this warming pasta bake topped with a cheese sauce.

1 Spray a large saucepan with the cooking spray and place over a medium heat. Add the onion, reduce the heat and cook for about 5 minutes until softened, adding a little water if the onion starts to stick. When the onion is soft, add the chillies and garlic and cook for 30 seconds or so. Add the tomatoes and oregano. Bring to the boil and simmer for 20–30 minutes until thickened. Season to taste and set aside.

2 Meanwhile, put the skimmed milk into another saucepan. Heat until warm but don't allow it to boil. Remove the pan from the heat and whisk in the sauce flour. Put the pan back over a medium heat and bring slowly to a simmer, whisking. Simmer for 2 minutes, whisking, then remove from the heat and add the Cheddar cheese. Stir until melted. Season and set aside.

3 Preheat the oven to Gas Mark 6/200°C/fan oven 180°C. Bring a large pan of water to the boil and cook the pasta according to the packet instructions, then drain thoroughly.

4 Stir the prawns into the tomato sauce, then add the pasta. Turn the mixture into a shallow ovenproof dish. Pour the cheese sauce over the top, then scatter with the cherry tomatoes, pressing them in slightly. Sprinkle with the Parmesan cheese.

5 Bake for 20–25 minutes. Remove from the oven and leave to stand for 10 minutes before serving.

Watercress and smoked salmon tagliatelle

Serves 4
567 calories per serving
Takes 15 minutes

225 g (8 oz) dried tagliatelle
500 g (1 lb 2 oz) asparagus spears, halved
calorie controlled cooking spray
100 g (3½ oz) low fat soft cheese with garlic and herbs
2 x 120 g packets smoked salmon trimmings
80 g (3 oz) watercress
freshly ground black pepper

Ready-flavoured low fat soft cheese with garlic and herbs makes an instant, and tasty, creamy sauce for pasta.

1 Bring a large pan of water to the boil and cook the pasta according to the packet instructions. Drain, reserving 8 tablespoons of the cooking liquid.

2 Heat a griddle pan until hot, spray the asparagus spears with the cooking spray and cook for 2–4 minutes, turning, until charred and softened.

3 Toss the asparagus, soft cheese, smoked salmon pieces and watercress together. Add the reserved cooking liquid and heat for 1–2 minutes until hot and the watercress has wilted. Stir into the pasta and serve with lots of freshly ground black pepper.

Pasta, pork and bean soup

Serves 4
335 calories per serving
Takes 30 minutes

**calorie controlled cooking
  spray**
**250 g (9 oz) lean pork, cubed
  finely**
1 red onion, chopped finely
2 garlic cloves, crushed
**2 sprigs fresh rosemary,
  leaves chopped**
**2 litres (3½ pints) chicken
  stock**
**400 g can red kidney beans,
  rinsed and drained**
**200 g (7 oz) small dried pasta
  shapes**
**salt and freshly ground black
  pepper**

*A thick and tasty soup in which the earthy flavour of
the rosemary perfectly complements the beans and the
sweetness of the pork.*

1 Heat a large non-stick saucepan and spray with the cooking
spray, then fry the pork over a high heat for 5 minutes until
golden brown. Add the onion, garlic, rosemary and seasoning
and stir-fry for another 5 minutes until the onion has softened.

2 Add the stock and bring to the boil. Add the beans and pasta
and simmer for 10 minutes. Check the seasoning, then serve.

Ⓥ **Variation…** For an equally satisfying vegetarian version
of this soup, omit the pork and use a vegetable stock.

Spaghetti marinara

Serves 4
505 calories per serving
Takes 35 minutes

calorie controlled cooking spray
2 onions, chopped
2 garlic cloves, chopped
2 x 400 g cans chopped tomatoes
25 g packet fresh oregano, chopped or 2 teaspoons dried oregano
1 teaspoon sugar
350 g (12 oz) dried spaghetti
2 x 200 g cans tuna steak in brine, drained
4 tablespoons olives, pitted and chopped
salt and freshly ground black pepper

'Marinara' is an Italian word meaning 'of the sea'. You'll find it applied to all sorts of tuna-based sauces. This is one of the easiest.

1 Spray a large frying pan with the cooking spray. Heat the pan, then fry the onions and garlic until softened – about 4 minutes.

2 Add the tomatoes, oregano, sugar and seasoning and cook for 20 minutes, stirring occasionally.

3 Bring a large pan of water to the boil and cook the pasta according to the packet instructions, then drain.

4 Add the tuna and olives to the tomatoes and cook for a further 5 minutes. Check the seasoning and serve the sauce with the spaghetti.

Smoked haddock macaroni cheese

Serves 4

438 calories per serving

Takes 20 minutes to prepare,
20 minutes to cook

450 ml (16 fl oz) skimmed milk
3 tablespoons cornflour
400 g (14 oz) smoked haddock
200 g (7 oz) dried macaroni
80 g (3 oz) half fat mature
Cheddar cheese, grated
2 tablespoons freshly grated
Parmesan cheese
2 spring onions, sliced
1 teaspoon Dijon mustard
(optional)
100 g (3½ oz) frozen peas
2 tomatoes, sliced

*Adding smoked haddock to basic macaroni cheese lifts
this dish to another level entirely.*

1 Preheat the oven to Gas Mark 6/200°C/fan oven 180°C.
Blend 4 tablespoons of the milk with the cornflour in a small
bowl and set it aside.

2 Pour the rest of the milk over the haddock in a large, lidded
pan. Cover and poach for 5 minutes. Remove the fish to a plate,
reserving the poaching liquid. Flake the fish roughly.

3 Meanwhile, bring a large pan of water to the boil and cook
the macaroni according to the packet instructions. Drain and
rinse in cold water.

4 Add the cornflour mixture to the poaching liquid and bring to
the boil, stirring until thickened. Mix the two cheeses together,
then measure out 30 g (1¼ oz) for the topping and mix with
the spring onions. Stir the rest of the cheese into the sauce,
plus the mustard, if using. Mix in the frozen peas, the smoked
haddock and the macaroni and transfer to an ovenproof dish.

5 Top with the sliced tomato and scatter with the cheese and
spring onion mixture. Bake in the oven for 20 minutes or until
bubbling and golden brown.

Pasta carbonara

Serves 4
318 calories per serving
Takes 20 minutes

250 g (9 oz) dried linguine or spaghetti
1 large leek, sliced thinly
calorie controlled cooking spray
4 rashers lean back bacon, snipped into pieces
2 garlic cloves, chopped finely
4 tablespoons skimmed milk
2 eggs, lightly beaten
½ teaspoon fresh lemon juice
2 tablespoons low fat soft cheese
salt and freshly ground black pepper
1 tablespoon chopped fresh parsley, to garnish (optional)

It's so easy to rustle up this comforting creamy pasta dish.

1 Bring a large pan of water to the boil and cook the pasta according to the packet instructions. Add the leek to the pasta for the last 2 minutes of cooking time. Drain the pasta and leek, then return them to the pan.

2 Meanwhile, spray a non-stick frying pan with the cooking spray and cook the bacon for 2 minutes until slightly crisp. Add the garlic and stir-fry for another minute, then add to the pasta and leek.

3 In a jug, beat together the milk and eggs and pour into the pan containing the pasta. Place on a medium heat and cook, stirring continuously with a wooden spoon, for 2 minutes.

4 Remove from the heat and stir in the lemon juice and soft cheese. Continue to stir off the heat for another minute. Season and serve in warm bowls sprinkled with parsley, if using.

Primavera pasta

Serves 4
400 calories per serving
Takes 30 minutes

200 g (7 oz) dried spaghetti

1.2 litres (2 pints) hot vegetable stock

1 medium onion, chopped finely

8 sprigs fresh thyme

2 large garlic cloves, sliced

150 g (5½ oz) baby carrots, trimmed

100 g (3½ oz) frozen petits pois

100 g (3½ oz) frozen broad beans

2 small courgettes, trimmed and sliced finely

100 g (3½ oz) fine asparagus spears, trimmed and cut into 2.5 cm (1 inch) pieces

8 tablespoons low fat soft cheese

2 egg yolks

salt and freshly ground black pepper

Enjoy tender spring vegetables with a hint of garlic and thyme in a quick creamy sauce.

1 Bring a large pan of water to the boil and cook the spaghetti according to the packet instructions, until al dente. Drain and return the spaghetti to the pan.

2 Meanwhile, in a separate saucepan, bring the vegetable stock to the boil and add the onion, thyme, garlic and carrots. Bring back to the boil and simmer for 5 minutes.

3 Add the petits pois, broad beans and courgettes to the stock. Bring back to the boil and simmer for 2 minutes. Add the asparagus and simmer for a further minute. Drain and add to the cooked spaghetti in the pan, reserving 200 ml (7 fl oz) of the cooking liquid.

4 Mix the reserved cooking liquid with the soft cheese and egg yolks. Return to the pan with the spaghetti and cook for 1 minute until slightly thickened. Season and serve immediately.

Roasted tomato spaghetti

Serves 4
320 calories per serving
Takes 25 minutes

calorie controlled cooking
  spray
**750 g (1 lb 10 oz) cherry
  tomatoes**
8 garlic cloves
**2 teaspoons extra virgin olive
  oil**
225 g (8 oz) dried spaghetti
**4 tablespoons shredded basil
  leaves**
**2 tablespoons balsamic
  vinegar**
**125 g packet light mozzarella
  cheese, drained and chopped
  roughly**
**salt and freshly ground black
  pepper**

*Don't be put off by the amount of garlic in this recipe:
when roasted, the cloves become sweet and lose
their pungency.*

1 Preheat the oven to Gas Mark 7/220°C/fan oven 200°C.
Line a roasting tin with foil and spray with the cooking spray.
Place the tomatoes and garlic in the tin, drizzle with the olive
oil, swirling the tin around to coat the tomatoes and roast for
20 minutes until the tomatoes are just charred and split.

2 Meanwhile, bring a large pan of water to the boil and cook
the pasta according to the packet instructions. Drain and rinse
thoroughly.

3 Remove the garlic cloves from the roasting tin and set
them aside to cool slightly. Mix the tomatoes, pasta and basil
together in the tin, season and reheat briefly in the oven.

4 Squeeze the garlic from its skin – it will be quite soft – and
mix with the balsamic vinegar. Stir the garlic mixture into the
pasta with the chopped mozzarella. Leave for 2 minutes so
that the heat melts the mozzarella, then serve.

Variation... Omit the mozzarella and serve sprinkled with
2 tablespoons of freshly grated Parmesan cheese.

Spaghetti Bolognese

Serves 4

330 calories per serving

Takes 15 minutes to prepare, 35 minutes to cook

calorie controlled cooking spray

1 green pepper, de-seeded and cubed

1 onion, cubed

1 garlic clove, chopped

225 g (8 oz) extra lean beef mince

1 courgette, cubed

1 large carrot, cubed

150 g (5½ oz) chestnut mushrooms

400 g can chopped tomatoes

2 tablespoons tomato purée

1 tablespoon chopped fresh marjoram

180 g (6 oz) dried spaghetti

salt and freshly ground black pepper

fresh basil leaves, to serve

This version is much lower in calories than the traditional family favourite – but no one will ever guess!

1 Spray a large saucepan with the cooking spray and add the green pepper, onion and garlic. Fry for 3–4 minutes, stirring occasionally, until they start to soften. Add the beef mince and fry for a further 6–8 minutes to brown the meat, stirring from time to time.

2 Add the courgette, carrot, mushrooms, canned tomatoes, tomato purée, marjoram and seasoning. Stir well before adding 200 ml (7 fl oz) of water. Stir again and bring to a simmer. Simmer for 20 minutes.

3 Bring a large saucepan of water to the boil and cook the spaghetti according to the packet instructions, until just tender.

4 Drain the spaghetti and divide between four warm plates or pasta bowls and spoon over the Bolognese sauce. Sprinkle with the basil and serve immediately.

Variation... Try using chicken or turkey mince for a change.

Vegetable pasta stew

Serves 4
375 calories per serving
Takes 35 minutes

calorie controlled cooking spray
1 onion, sliced
2 garlic cloves, sliced
200 g (7 oz) turnips, quartered
200 g (7 oz) Chantenay carrots, trimmed
200 g (7 oz) baby parsnips, peeled and trimmed, or larger parsnips, peeled and cut into chunks
150 g (5½ oz) mushrooms, halved
200 g (7 oz) dried conchiglie (pasta shells)
700 ml (1¼ pints) hot vegetable stock
125 ml (4 fl oz) red wine
2 rosemary sprigs
4 thyme sprigs
2 bay leaves
400 g can borlotti beans, drained and rinsed
110 g (4 oz) green beans, chopped
2 tablespoons half fat crème fraîche

This hearty winter stew is packed with root vegetables and a delicious creamy broth.

1 Spray a large, lidded saucepan with the cooking spray. Heat over a medium heat until sizzling, then add the onion and garlic. Cook for 5 minutes until softened, adding a splash of water if they start to stick. Add the turnips, carrots, parsnips and mushrooms. Cook, stirring, for 5 minutes until just beginning to brown.

2 Add the pasta, stock, red wine and herbs. Bring to the boil, cover and simmer for 10 minutes, stirring occasionally.

3 Add the borlotti and green beans. Cook for 5 minutes until all the vegetables are tender and the pasta is cooked. Remove the bay leaves and stir in the crème fraîche. Bring the stew back to the boil to warm through before serving.

Tip... If you want a lighter stew, omit the crème fraîche.

Roasted red pepper beef pasta

Serves 4
444 calories per serving
Takes 28 minutes
❄ (meat sauce only)

3 red peppers, halved and
   de-seeded
calorie controlled cooking
   spray
1 onion, cubed finely
2 garlic cloves, crushed
450 g (1 lb oz) lean beef mince
2 tablespoons tomato purée
1 tablespoon Worcestershire
   sauce
2 tablespoons fresh thyme
   leaves
250 g (9 oz) dried penne pasta
15 g (½ oz) Parmesan cheese,
   grated
salt and freshly ground black
   pepper

*Charring the peppers adds real depth of flavour – the
sauce tastes as if it's been slow-cooked for hours.*

1 Preheat the grill to high. Put the pepper halves on a grill tray,
skin side up, and grill for 10 minutes until the skin is blackened
and charred. Transfer to a bowl and cover with cling film.

2 Meanwhile, heat a wide, lidded, non-stick saucepan sprayed
with the cooking spray and add the onion, garlic and mince.
Cook for 5 minutes, breaking up the mince, until browned.
Stir in the tomato purée, Worcestershire sauce and thyme.
Continue to cook, uncovered, for 1 minute, then cover and
continue to cook gently for 10 minutes.

3 Bring a large pan of water to the boil and cook the pasta
according to the packet instructions, until al dente. Add a
ladleful of the pasta cooking liquid to the mince mixture, then
drain the pasta.

4 Peel the skin from the peppers and place half of the peppers
in a food processor. Whizz until smooth. Finely cube the
remaining peppers.

5 Stir all the peppers and seasoning into the beef mixture
and cook for 1 minute. Add the pasta and toss to coat. Divide
between warm plates, top with the cheese and serve.

Welsh leek and cheese pasta bake

Serves 4

433 calories per serving

Takes 20 minutes to prepare,
20 minutes to cook

250 g (9 oz) dried penne

**calorie controlled cooking
spray**

**500 g (1 lb 2 oz) leeks,
trimmed and sliced**

40 g (1½ oz) cornflour

600 ml (20 fl oz) skimmed milk

**½ vegetable stock cube,
crumbled**

freshly grated nutmeg

**3 tablespoons snipped fresh
chives**

**100 g (3½ oz) Caerphilly
cheese, grated**

freshly ground black pepper

*A hint of nutmeg adds a delicate flavour to the cheese
sauce in this comforting dish.*

1 Preheat the oven to Gas Mark 6/200°C/fan oven 180°C.
Bring a large pan of water to the boil and cook the pasta
according to the packet instructions. Drain and rinse in
cold water.

2 Meanwhile, heat a lidded, non-stick saucepan and spray
with the cooking spray. Cook the leeks for 1 minute then add
4 tablespoons of water, cover the pan and cook gently for
5–6 minutes. Tip the leeks out on to a plate.

3 Use the same saucepan to make the sauce. Blend the
cornflour with a little of the milk until you have a smooth paste.
Gradually blend in the rest of the milk and add the crumbled
stock cube. Bring to the boil, stirring, and simmer for 2 minutes.
Season with black pepper and nutmeg.

4 Mix the chives and cheese together, then stir half into the
sauce. Mix the sauce with the drained pasta and tip into an
ovenproof baking dish. Spoon the leeks on top and scatter the
rest of the cheese and chives all over. Bake for 20 minutes
until golden brown.

Tuna lasagne

Serves 4

390 calories per serving

Takes 35 minutes to prepare,
50 minutes to cook

❄

calorie controlled cooking
spray

1 large onion, chopped

2 garlic cloves, crushed

2 courgettes, sliced

140 g (5 oz) frozen or canned
sweetcorn, drained

400 g can chopped tomatoes

200 g can tuna in brine,
drained and flaked

50 g (1¾ oz) low fat spread

3 tablespoons plain flour

1 teaspoon mustard powder

450 ml (16 fl oz) skimmed milk

8 lasagne sheets

40 g (1½ oz) half fat Cheddar
cheese, grated

salt and freshly ground black
pepper

*A pleasant change from meat lasagne, this recipe is slightly
lighter and very flavoursome. Serve with a chunky tomato
and cucumber salad.*

1 Spray a medium saucepan with the cooking spray and fry
the onion and garlic for 4–5 minutes, until softened. Add the
sliced courgettes, sweetcorn and chopped tomatoes and cook,
uncovered, for 15 minutes. Stir in the flaked tuna.

2 Preheat the oven to Gas Mark 6/ 200°C/fan oven 180°C.
Melt the low fat spread in a small saucepan. Add the flour and
mustard powder, and stir well for 1 minute.

3 Gradually add the milk and whisk after every addition.
Continue whisking until the sauce is thick and smooth.
Season well.

4 Spoon one third of the tuna and courgette mixture into a
shallow ovenproof baking dish and top with half the lasagne
sheets. Spoon in another third of the tuna mixture and cover
with the remaining lasagne sheets. Top with the remaining
tuna mixture.

5 Pour over the white sauce and top with the grated cheese.
Bake in the oven for 45–50 minutes, until the top is golden
and bubbling.

 Variation… For a vegetarian option, omit the tuna
and add a 400 g can of kidney beans and use half fat
vegetarian Cheddar cheese.

Speedy suppers

Crab and rocket linguine

Serves 1
414 calories per serving
Takes 10 minutes

75 g (2¾ oz) dried linguine, snapped in half
1 spring onion, chopped finely
½ red chilli, de-seeded and chopped finely
1 garlic clove, chopped finely
grated zest and juice of ½ a lime
170 g can white crab meat in brine, drained
a handful of rocket leaves
salt and freshly ground black pepper

Spoil yourself with this speedy but incredibly tasty pasta dish for one.

1 Bring a large pan of water to the boil and cook the pasta according to the packet instructions. Drain, reserving a mugful of the pasta water.

2 Return the pasta to the pan and toss it really well with the spring onion, chilli, garlic and lime zest, adding a little of the pasta water to loosen the texture. Gently toss in the crab, add the lime juice and season. Serve topped with the rocket leaves.

Variation… You could also add 50 g (1¾ oz) frozen peas in step 1. When the pasta has cooked for 5 minutes, add the peas, return to the boil and cook for 2 minutes more.

Tagliatelle with Parmesan

Serves 3
380 calories per serving
Takes 10 minutes

250 g (9 oz) fresh tagliatelle
100 g (3½ oz) low fat soft cheese with onions and chives
3 tablespoons freshly grated Parmesan cheese
freshly ground black pepper
a handful of fresh chives, snipped, to garnish

A very quick and easy dish for when you're in a hurry.

1 Bring a large pan of water to the boil and cook the tagliatelle according to the packet instructions.

2 Meanwhile, in a small saucepan, gently melt the soft cheese.

3 Drain the tagliatelle, toss all the ingredients together and season well with black pepper. Serve immediately, scattered with the snipped chives.

Variation… Look out for vegetarian Parmesan at the supermarket if cooking for vegetarians.

Creamy leek and mushroom pasta

Serves 1
301 calories per serving
Takes 12 minutes

60 g (2 oz) dried penne
110 g (4 oz) leeks, sliced
calorie controlled cooking
  spray
110 g (4 oz) mushrooms,
  chopped roughly
1 garlic clove, crushed
1 teaspoon chopped fresh
  thyme
40 g (1½ oz) low fat soft
  cheese
salt and freshly ground black
  pepper

Low fat soft cheese makes a deliciously creamy sauce for pasta, with extra flavour from the garlic and thyme.

1 Bring a large pan of water to the boil and cook the penne according to the packet instructions.

2 Meanwhile, coat the sliced leeks in the cooking spray in a lidded non-stick saucepan. Add seasoning and 2 tablespoons water, cover the pan and cook for 3 minutes.

3 Add the mushrooms, garlic and thyme to the leeks, cover the pan and cook for 5 minutes. Stir the low fat soft cheese into the juices to make a creamy sauce.

4 Drain the pasta and toss with the sauce. Serve immediately in a warm bowl.

Italian sardine pasta

Serves 4
440 calories per serving
Takes 15 minutes

350 g (12 oz) dried pasta

2 x 120 g cans sardines in brine, drained and flaked

250 g (9 oz) cherry tomatoes, halved

juice and zest of a lemon

1 red chilli, de-seeded and chopped finely

25 g packet fresh basil, chopped

salt and freshly ground black pepper

The fastest way ever to put together this classic Italian combination of flavours.

1 Bring a large pan of water to the boil and cook the pasta according to the packet instructions.

2 Meanwhile heat a large pan and add the sardines, tomatoes, lemon juice and zest, chilli and seasoning. Heat the ingredients through gently, stirring occasionally, for 4 minutes. Drain the pasta and toss with the sardines and tomato mixture and the fresh basil. Serve immediately in warm bowls.

Courgette, pesto and lemon pasta

Serves 1
302 calories per serving
Takes 15 minutes

½ tablespoon pine nut kernels
40 g (1½ oz) dried spirali
calorie controlled cooking
   spray
1 courgette, sliced thinly
a pinch of dried chilli flakes
25 g (1 oz) sun-dried tomatoes
   in oil, drained and chopped
   roughly
2 teaspoons red pesto
zest of ½ a lemon
½ tablespoon finely grated
   Parmesan cheese
salt and freshly ground black
   pepper

This easy vegetarian dish has the merest hint of chilli and a sprinkling of toasted pine nut kernels.

1 Dry fry the pine nut kernels in a non-stick frying pan for 2–3 minutes until golden and toasted. Bring a large pan of water to the boil and cook the according to the packet instructions, until al dente. Drain well.

2 Meanwhile, spray a non-stick frying pan with the cooking spray and place over a high heat. Add the courgette slices and cook for 4–5 minutes until golden. Add the chilli flakes and cook briefly.

3 Return the pasta to the pan and add the courgette slices, sun-dried tomatoes, pine nut kernels, pesto and lemon zest. Season to taste and stir well.

4 Transfer to a warm plate and sprinkle with the Parmesan cheese. Serve immediately.

Tomato, asparagus and basil fusilli

Serves 2
267 calories per serving
Takes 15 minutes

125 g (4½ oz) dried fusilli
100 g (3½ oz) asparagus tips
calorie controlled cooking
  spray
1 garlic clove, crushed
250 g (9 oz) cherry tomatoes,
  halved
½ teaspoon caster sugar
2 heaped tablespoons
  shredded fresh basil
freshly ground black pepper

*If you're looking for a supper that can be made from
scratch in just a matter of minutes, try this speedy
vegetarian pasta dish.*

1 Bring a large pan of water to the boil and cook the pasta
according to the packet instructions, adding the asparagus tips
for the last 4 minutes of cooking time.

2 Meanwhile, spray a lidded saucepan with cooking spray.
Add the garlic and tomatoes and fry for 1 minute until starting
to soften. Season with black pepper and stir in the sugar. Cover
and cook for 4 minutes until the tomatoes form a sauce.

3 Drain the pasta and asparagus and toss together with the
tomato sauce and the basil. Serve immediately.

Smoked salmon linguine

Serves 2
358 calories per serving
Takes 15 minutes

125 g (4½ oz) dried linguine
1 egg
60 g (2 oz) low fat soft cheese
finely grated zest and juice of
½ a small lemon
2 tablespoons snipped fresh
chives
60 g (2 oz) smoked salmon,
sliced into strips
freshly ground black pepper

Serve with a mixed leaf and rocket salad, dressed with a little lemon juice.

1 Bring a large pan of water to the boil and cook the pasta according to the packet instructions.

2 Meanwhile, in a small bowl, beat the egg with the soft cheese, then stir in the lemon zest and juice, chives and smoked salmon.

3 Drain the pasta and return to the saucepan. Add the smoked salmon mixture, tossing well to mix thoroughly. Season with black pepper and serve in warmed bowls.

Tip... Smoked salmon trimmings are perfect for this recipe, and cost a lot less than sliced smoked salmon.

Chick pea and tomato pasta

Serves 2
316 calories per serving
Takes 30 minutes

110 g (4 oz) dried fusilli
calorie controlled cooking spray
75 g (2¾ oz) mushrooms, sliced
400 g can chopped tomatoes with herbs
150 g (5½ oz) canned chick peas, drained
2 teaspoons smoked paprika

Canned chick peas are a great storecupboard standby for this simple pasta supper.

1 Bring a large pan of water to the boil and cook the pasta according to the packet instructions. Drain and keep warm.

2 Meanwhile, heat a large frying pan, spray with the cooking spray and cook the mushrooms for 3–5 minutes until golden. Add the tomatoes, chick peas and paprika, reduce the heat and simmer for 10 minutes. Toss the pasta into the sauce and serve immediately.

Crispy turkey rasher pasta

Serves 4
390 calories per serving
Takes 20 minutes

350 g (12 oz) dried farfalle pasta
150 g (5½ oz) turkey rashers

For the salsa
2 green chillies, de-seeded and chopped finely
1 green pepper, de-seeded and chopped finely
1 onion, chopped finely
125 g can chopped tomatoes
2 teaspoons sugar
1 tablespoon white wine vinegar
salt and freshly ground black pepper

A piquant pepper salsa makes this supper dish into something special.

1 Bring a large pan of water to the boil and cook the pasta according to the packet instructions.

2 Meanwhile, preheat the grill to high and cook the turkey rashers until crispy – 1 minute on each side – then slice into bite size pieces.

3 In a bowl mix together all the salsa ingredients with some seasoning. Drain the cooked pasta and toss with the turkey rashers and salsa. Check the seasoning and serve.

Walnut pasta twists

Serves 2
390 calories per serving
Takes 15 minutes

**600 ml (20 fl oz) vegetable
stock**
**125 g (4½ oz) dried small
pasta shapes, such as spirali**
**25 g packet fresh basil, leaves
only**
**½ x 25 g packet fresh parsley,
leaves chopped**
30 g (1¼ oz) walnut pieces
1 garlic clove, crushed
**25 g (1 oz) Parmesan cheese,
grated**
**salt and freshly ground black
pepper**

*Serve each bowl with a warm 30 g (1¼ oz) slice of French
bread per person and a generous mixed salad.*

1 Put the vegetable stock in a saucepan and bring to the boil.
Add the pasta and cook according to the packet instructions,
until al dente.

2 Meanwhile, whizz the basil, parsley, walnuts and garlic in a
food processor until finely chopped. Reserve a ladleful of the
pasta cooking liquid in a jug and drain the pasta.

3 Return the pasta to the pan and stir in the reserved cooking
liquid, the walnut mixture and the cheese. Stir to coat the pasta
and heat through. Check the seasoning and serve.

Variation… Add 100 g (3½ oz) cooked, shredded, skinless
chicken in step 3 and gently heat until piping hot.

Courgette and cherry tomato pasta

Serves 1

444 calories per serving

Takes 20 minutes

100 g (3½ oz) dried tagliatelle

calorie controlled cooking spray

2 spring onions, sliced

1 small courgette, sliced thinly into ribbons with a vegetable peeler

125 g (4½ oz) cherry tomatoes, halved

50 g (1¾ oz) virtually fat free fromage frais

½ tablespoon chopped fresh parsley

½ tablespoon chopped fresh mint

½ tablespoon chopped fresh chives

salt and freshly ground black pepper

A very tasty, summery dish, with fresh herbs that add lots of flavour.

1 Bring a large pan of water to the boil and cook the pasta according to the packet instructions, until al dente.

2 Meanwhile, heat the cooking spray in a frying pan. Add the spring onions and courgette ribbons and cook over a medium heat, stirring occasionally, for 3–4 minutes. Add the cherry tomatoes and cook for a further 2–3 minutes before stirring in the fromage frais. Season well.

3 Drain the pasta and return to the pan. Stir the herbs into the courgettes and cherry tomatoes and pour the mixture into the pasta pan. Toss together gently and serve.

Creamy beef and mushroom pasta

Serves 2
445 calories per serving
Takes 15–20 minutes

175 g (6 oz) rump steak, fat removed

calorie controlled cooking spray

110 g (4 oz) chestnut mushrooms, sliced

2 garlic cloves, sliced

100 ml (3½ fl oz) hot beef stock

60 g (2 oz) low fat soft cheese

1 tablespoon chopped fresh tarragon, plus extra to garnish

200 g (7 oz) fresh tagliatelle

salt and freshly ground black pepper

This is a really quick supper dish and it's delicious with a green salad.

1 Season the steak on both sides. Heat a medium non-stick frying pan until hot. Add the steak and fry for 2–4 minutes on each side, depending on how well done you like it. Remove from the pan, cover with foil and leave to rest.

2 Spray the pan with the cooking spray and add the mushrooms. Cook for 5 minutes until the juices released have evaporated. Add the garlic and cook for a further 1 minute. Add the stock, bring to the boil and simmer for 2 minutes before stirring in the soft cheese. Reduce the heat and warm through, stirring in the tarragon and seasoning.

3 Meanwhile, bring a large pan of water to the boil and cook the pasta according to the packet instructions. Drain well.

4 Slice the steak into thin strips and add to the sauce, along with any juices. Refresh and warm the pasta by running very hot water over it in the colander. Serve the pasta in warm bowls with the steak and sauce on top. Garnish with a little tarragon.

Ⓥ **Variation…** For a vegetarian version, use vegetable stock, omit the steak and stir in 110 g (4 oz) Quorn Deli Style Ham, cut into strips, with the stock.

Mushroom and ham tagliatelle

Serves 2
365 calories per serving
Takes 15–20 minutes

175 g (6 oz) dried tagliatelle
calorie controlled cooking spray
200 g (7 oz) mushrooms, sliced
juice of ½ a lemon
3 tablespoons virtually fat free fromage frais
150 g (5½ oz) lean ham, all fat removed, cut into strips
salt and freshly ground black pepper
a small bunch of chives, snipped finely, to garnish (optional)

Serve with a big crunchy salad of crisp lettuce, cherry tomatoes and red pepper strips, seasoned and drizzled with a little balsamic vinegar.

1 Bring a large pan of water to the boil and cook the pasta according to the packet instructions.

2 Meanwhile, heat a large frying pan and spray with the cooking spray. Add the mushrooms, season and stir-fry on a high heat for 3 minutes until they are soft and have re-absorbed all their juices. Add the lemon juice, then add 100 ml (3½ fl oz) cold water and stir, scraping up any juices stuck to the pan. Take the pan off the heat and stir in the fromage frais, ham and seasoning.

3 Drain the pasta, reserving a few tablespoons of the cooking liquid. Toss the pasta in the ham and mushroom sauce with the reserved liquid and check the seasoning. Serve garnished with snipped chives, if using.

Tip… When making pasta sauces, always try to reserve a few tablespoons of the pasta cooking liquid to add to the sauce. It improves the texture of the sauce and helps to bind it to the pasta.

Creamy sausage and mustard pasta

Serves 4
565 calories per serving
Takes 20 minutes

350 g (12 oz) dried pasta
ribbons (e.g. parpadelle or
tagliatelle)
454 g packet reduced fat thick
pork sausages
1 garlic clove, chopped finely
250 g (9 oz) mushrooms,
sliced
2 tablespoons Dijon or
wholegrain mustard
juice of a lemon
2 tablespoons half fat crème
fraîche
25 g packet fresh flat leaf
parsley, chopped
salt and freshly ground black
pepper

*This dish uses lots of parsley to counterbalance the rich
creamy sauce.*

1 Bring a large pan of water to the boil and cook the pasta
according to the packet instructions. Drain well.

2 Meanwhile, remove the meat from the sausages and
brown the sausagemeat in a large frying pan. Add the garlic,
mushrooms and seasoning.

3 When the mushrooms are cooked, add the mustard, lemon
juice and 2 tablespoons of water and heat through. Remove
the pan from the heat and stir in the crème fraîche. Check the
seasoning. Serve with the pasta and sprinkle with the parsley.

Pasta with pesto sauce

Serves 4
255 calories per serving
Takes 20 minutes

175 g (6 oz) dried spaghetti, linguine or tagliatelle
20 g (¾ oz) pine nut kernels
40 g (1½ oz) fresh basil leaves
2 tablespoons extra virgin olive oil
salt and freshly ground black pepper

Making your own pesto is easy in a food processor – and it tastes so much nicer than shop-bought.

1 Bring a large pan of water to the boil, and cook the pasta according to the packet instructions.

2 Meanwhile, heat a small non-stick frying pan until hot, add the pine nut kernels and dry fry over a medium heat for 1–2 minutes, stirring until golden all over. Place the basil, olive oil, pine nut kernels and a pinch of salt in a food processor or liquidiser and blend briefly to a paste.

3 Drain the pasta, reserving 4 tablespoons of the cooking liquid, and rinse thoroughly. Return the pasta to the pan with the pesto sauce and reserved cooking liquid. Stir through, season and serve immediately.

Tips… The heat from the pasta is enough to warm the pesto.

The pesto will keep, covered, in the fridge for a week.

Variation… Make a basil and roasted pepper pesto by adding 2 drained and chopped roasted peppers in vinegar, from a jar, to the blender.

Fresh tomato pasta

Serves 4
375 calories per serving
Takes 20 minutes

350 g (12 oz) dried pasta
calorie controlled cooking
  spray
1 onion, chopped roughly
2 garlic cloves, crushed
1 kg (2 lb 4 oz) ripe tomatoes,
  chopped roughly
25 g packet fresh basil or
  parsley, chopped
salt and freshly ground black
  pepper

*This is the opposite of a long, slow-cooked pasta sauce
and is hardly cooked at all. It also makes an excellent
topping for a ready-made pizza base.*

1 Bring a large pan of water to the boil and cook the pasta
according to the packet instructions.

2 Meanwhile, spray a large frying pan with the cooking spray
and put it on a medium heat. Stir-fry the onion and garlic until
soft – about 4 minutes – and then add the tomatoes. Season.
Cook for about 15 minutes on a medium heat or until the
tomatoes have broken down.

3 Drain the pasta and toss it in the sauce with the fresh basil
or parsley, and serve.

Smoked mackerel pasta

Serves 2
456 calories per serving
Takes 20 minutes

110 g (4 oz) dried wholemeal
  pasta shapes, e.g. penne
50 g (1¾ oz) broccoli florets
110 g (4 oz) smoked mackerel
  fillets, skinned and flaked
3 small vine-ripened tomatoes,
  quartered

For the pesto sauce
1 tablespoon pine nut kernels
25 g (1 oz) basil leaves
1 tablespoon finely grated
  Parmesan cheese
1 garlic clove

This pasta dish is packed with robust flavours that go surprisingly well together.

1 Bring a large pan of water to the boil and cook the pasta according to the packet instructions. Add the broccoli florets for the final 4 minutes of cooking time. Drain well and return to the pan.

2 Skin and flake the mackerel and add to the pasta and broccoli in the pan, along with the tomatoes.

3 To make the pesto, toast the pine nut kernels by dry-frying them in a frying pan for a couple of minutes until they begin to brown. Then place all the ingredients in a small blender and whizz to a paste. Add 2 tablespoons of warm water and blend again.

4 Pour the pesto sauce into the pasta mixture, stir well and heat through over a low heat until piping hot.

Tip... You can use 2 tablespoons of ready-made reduced fat pesto if you don't have the ingredients for home-made pesto to hand.

Linguine with broad beans and rocket

Serves 1
307 calories per serving
Takes 20 minutes

60 g (2 oz) shelled broad
  beans, defrosted if frozen
60 g (2 oz) dried linguine
calorie controlled cooking
  spray
1 garlic clove, chopped finely
2 tablespoons low fat soft
  cheese
1 tablespoon lemon juice
25 g (1 oz) rocket leaves
salt and freshly ground black
  pepper

Make the most of broad beans in season – or use frozen ones later in the year.

1 Bring a saucepan of water to the boil, add the broad beans and cook for 2 minutes, then refresh under cold water. When cool, slip them out of their grey outer shells to reveal the bright green beans inside.

2 Meanwhile, bring another large pan of water to the boil and cook the pasta according to the packet instructions, until al dente. Drain, reserving 2 tablespoons of the cooking water.

3 Heat a non-stick frying pan and spray with the cooking spray. Cook the garlic for 1 minute, then stir in the soft cheese, lemon juice and reserved pasta cooking water. Add the pasta and broad beans, and toss until combined and warmed through.

4 Remove from the heat and stir in the rocket and season before serving.

Penne pasta with prawns and basil

Serves 2
355 calories per serving
Takes 20 minutes

125 g (4½ oz) dried penne

2 courgettes, quartered
lengthways and sliced
into chunks

calorie controlled cooking
spray

1 teaspoon olive oil

3 garlic cloves, crushed

1 red chilli, de-seeded and
sliced thinly

200 g (7 oz) frozen raw king
prawns, defrosted

1 tablespoon lemon juice

a handful of fresh basil leaves,
torn

salt and freshly ground black
pepper

Prawns and pasta are a great fast-supper combination.

1 Bring a large pan of water to the boil and cook the pasta according to the packet instructions. Add the courgettes for the last 2 minutes of cooking time and return to the boil. Drain.

2 Meanwhile, heat a large non-stick frying pan. Spray with the cooking spray, then add the oil, garlic, chilli and prawns and fry for 3 minutes, stirring regularly until the prawns are pink.

3 Drain the pasta and courgettes, reserving 3 tablespoons of the cooking water. Add the pasta, courgettes, reserved cooking water and lemon juice to the prawns and warm through for 1 minute. Season and divide between two plates. Scatter with the torn basil.

Tip… Instead of raw prawns, use ready cooked ones, tossing them in at the end of step 3.

Variation… Swap the prawns for 150 g (5½ oz) canned chick peas, drained and rinsed. Add them to the pan with the garlic in step 2.

Quick tomato tuna pasta

Serves 4
465 calories per serving
Takes 20 minutes

350 g (12 oz) dried pasta
  shapes
calorie controlled cooking
  spray
1 large onion, chopped
2 garlic cloves, crushed
2 x 400 g cans chopped
  tomatoes
2 x 150 g cans tuna steaks
  in brine, drained
1 teaspoon dried oregano
20 stoned olives in brine,
  drained and halved
  (optional)
salt and freshly ground black
  pepper
a small bunch of fresh parsley
  or basil, chopped, to garnish
  (optional)

This is a staple family meal: all the ingredients are in the storecupboard and it can be on the table in 20 minutes.

1 Bring a large pan of water to the boil and cook the pasta according to the packet instructions.

2 Meanwhile, spray a large frying-pan with the cooking spray and fry the onion and garlic for about 5 minutes until softened, adding a few tablespoons of water if they begin to stick.

3 Add the tomatoes, tuna, oregano, olives (if using) and seasoning. Stir together and break the tuna into chunks. Bring the sauce to the boil, then simmer for 15 minutes until thick.

4 Drain the pasta, reserving 4 tablespoons of the cooking water and add to the sauce with the water. Stir together until well coated with the sauce, then serve, sprinkled with fresh herbs, if using.

Variation… Turn this dish into a special treat with 2 x 150 g (5½ oz) fresh tuna steaks instead. Grill them first and flake them into the finished sauce before tossing with the pasta.

Tagliatelle with mussels

Serves 4
225 calories per serving
Takes 20 minutes

1 kg (2 lb 4 oz) live mussels
   in their shells, cleaned
4 tablespoons dry white wine
150 ml (5 fl oz) fish stock
1 garlic clove, crushed
3 tablespoons chopped fresh
   parsley
250 g (9 oz) fresh tagliatelle
1 tablespoon olive oil
400 g can chopped tomatoes
2 tablespoons tomato purée
chopped fresh parsley, to
   garnish

Cook this dish for supper and imagine you're on holiday in the Med.

1 Place the cleaned mussels in a large pan with the wine, stock, garlic and parsley. Cover the pan and cook for 5 minutes, until the mussels have opened. Discard any mussels that haven't opened.

2 Bring a large pan of water to the boil and cook the pasta according to the packet instructions. Drain well.

3 Heat the olive oil in a pan and add the chopped tomatoes and tomato purée. Drain the mussels, reserving the cooking liquid. Add the cooking liquid to the tomatoes. Allow to bubble for 2–3 minutes, then toss in the cooked pasta and mussels. Pile on to warm plates and scatter with a little extra chopped parsley. Serve at once.

Tips… If you prefer, remove the mussels from their shells before tossing them into the pasta.

Look out for bags of cleaned live mussels in the supermarkets.

Beef, rocket and tomato pasta

Serves 4
314 calories per serving
Takes 25 minutes

300 g (10½ oz) lean beef rump
  steak
calorie controlled cooking
  spray
400 g (14 oz) vine-ripened
  tomatoes, halved
3 tablespoons balsamic
  vinegar
225 g (8 oz) dried tagliatelle
2 large garlic cloves, sliced
  thinly
50 g (1¾ oz) rocket leaves
salt and freshly ground black
  pepper

Roasting the tomatoes with balsamic vinegar boosts their flavour in this classic combination.

1 Preheat the oven to Gas Mark 6/200°C/fan oven 180°C. Heat a large non-stick frying pan until hot and spray the steak with the cooking spray. Cook for 1–2 minutes on each side until browned.

2 Transfer the steak to a small roasting tray and scatter the tomatoes around it. Spray again with the cooking spray and drizzle over 1 tablespoon of the balsamic vinegar. Roast for 10 minutes, or until the steak is cooked to your liking and the tomatoes have softened. Leave to rest for 5 minutes, then thinly slice the steak and keep warm with the tomatoes.

3 Meanwhile, bring a large pan of water to the boil and cook the pasta according to the packet instructions. Once cooked, drain, reserving 6 tablespoons of the cooking liquid.

4 Spray the frying pan again with the cooking spray and cook the garlic for 1 minute. Add any juices from the roasting tray, the remaining balsamic vinegar and the reserved cooking liquid and cook for 2 minutes or until reduced.

5 Add the steak to the frying pan along with the tomatoes and tagliatelle. Continue to heat gently, tossing to combine, until warmed through. Remove from the heat and toss in the rocket. Season and serve in large shallow bowls.

Broccoli, pancetta and lemon pasta

Serves 4
280 calories per serving
Takes 20 minutes

200 g (7 oz) broccoli, cut into small florets
200 g (7 oz) dried conchiglie (pasta shells)
zest and juice of a lemon
50 g (1¾ oz) cubetti di pancetta
1 garlic clove, crushed
100 g (3½ oz) half fat crème fraîche
salt and freshly ground black pepper

Cubetti di pancetta is cubed Italian cured bacon – it adds a real kick to this dish.

1 Bring a large pan of water to the boil. Add the broccoli and cook for 3 minutes. Remove the broccoli from the pan using a slotted spoon and leave it to drain in a colander set over a bowl. Keep the water on the heat.

2 Add the pasta to the pan along with the lemon juice and return it to the boil. Cook according to the packet instructions, until al dente.

3 Meanwhile, finely chop the broccoli florets into small pieces. Heat a non-stick frying pan and cook the pancetta for 3 minutes until crispy. Remove from the heat and stir in the garlic, broccoli and lemon zest.

4 Drain the pasta and return to the pan. Stir in the broccoli mixture and crème fraîche and gently heat until warmed through. Check the seasoning and serve immediately.

Variation… Replace the pancetta with 2–3 tablespoons of chopped fresh parsley, chives or basil.

Spaghetti with meatballs

Serves 4
331 calories per serving
Takes 30 minutes
❄ (for the sauce and
   meatballs)

300 g (10½ oz) extra lean beef
   mince
calorie controlled cooking
   spray
1 onion, chopped finely
1 red pepper, de-seeded and
   cut into thin strips
1 yellow pepper, de-seeded
   and cut into thin strips
400 g can chopped tomatoes
   with herbs and garlic
200 g (7 oz) dried spaghetti
salt and freshly ground black
   pepper

*No need to buy ready-made meatballs: it only takes a few
minutes to shape your own.*

1 Season the mince with salt and freshly ground black pepper.
Shape into 16–20 walnut size meatballs. Spray a non-stick
frying pan with the cooking spray and heat until hot. Add the
meatballs and cook, turning, for 5 minutes until browned.
Remove from the pan and set aside.

2 Re-spray the pan with cooking spray, add the onion and
peppers and stir-fry for 4 minutes until tender. Add the
tomatoes and 4 tablespoons of water and stir to mix. Return
the meatballs to the pan, reduce the heat and leave to simmer
for 10–15 minutes until cooked through.

3 Meanwhile, bring a large pan of water to the boil and cook
the pasta according to the packet instructions. Drain and divide
between four warm bowls. Top with the meatballs and sauce,
and serve.

A touch of spice

Pasta puttanesca

Serves 4
253 calories per serving
Takes 20 minutes

❄ (sauce only)

250 g (9 oz) dried spaghetti

calorie controlled cooking spray

1 large garlic clove, chopped finely

400 g can cherry tomatoes or chopped tomatoes

1 teaspoon dried oregano

60 g (2 oz) stoned black olives in brine, halved

¼–½ teaspoon dried chilli flakes (optional)

1 tablespoon small capers in brine, drained

salt and freshly ground black pepper

1 tablespoon chopped fresh parsley, to garnish

This is a vegetarian version of the classic Italian pasta sauce, which normally contains anchovies. For a genuine puttanesca sauce, add 25 g (1 oz) anchovies.

1 Bring a large pan of water to the boil and cook the pasta according to the packet instructions.

2 Meanwhile, heat a large, non-stick frying pan and spray liberally with the cooking spray. Add the garlic and cook for 1 minute, then stir in the tomatoes, oregano, olives, chilli flakes (if using) and capers. Bring to the boil, then reduce the heat and simmer for 5 minutes.

3 Drain the cooked pasta, reserving 3 tablespoons of the cooking liquid. Stir the reserved cooking liquid into the frying pan, add the drained pasta, stir and season to taste. Sprinkle with the parsley before serving.

Fiery garlic pasta

Serves 4

395 calories per serving

Takes 15 minutes

350 g (12 oz) dried spaghetti

4 garlic cloves, chopped

2 tablespoons olive oil

2 red chillies, de-seeded and chopped finely or 1 teaspoon dried chilli flakes

zest and juice of a lemon

25 g packet fresh parsley, chopped

salt and freshly ground black pepper

If you love garlic and spicy food then this is your fast-food pasta heaven.

1 Bring a large pan of water to the boil and cook the pasta according to the packet instructions. Drain.

2 Meanwhile, heat a large non-stick frying pan or wok and fry the garlic in the olive oil until golden. Add the chillies or chilli flakes and remove the pan from the heat.

3 When the pasta is ready, drain it and toss it in the hot oil. Add the lemon zest, juice, chopped parsley and seasoning, and serve straight away.

Spicy tomato tagliatelle

Serves 1
210 calories per serving
Takes 25 minutes

40 g (1½ oz) dried tagliatelle
calorie controlled cooking
   spray
2 spring onions, chopped
140 g (5 oz) red and yellow
   cherry tomatoes, preferably
   on the vine
½ red chilli, de-seeded and
   cubed
1 tablespoon chopped fresh
   parsley
salt and freshly ground black
   pepper
1 tablespoon freshly grated
   Parmesan cheese, to serve

*This wonderfully simple and tasty dish brings out the fresh,
sweet flavour of cherry tomatoes.*

1 Bring a large pan of water to the boil and cook the pasta
according to the packet instructions. Drain and rinse.

2 Meanwhile, spray a saucepan with the cooking spray and
heat until sizzling. Add the spring onions and cook over a
medium heat until just beginning to brown.

3 Add the tomatoes to the pan with the chilli. Cook over a low
heat for 5 minutes, adding a little water if necessary, until they
have softened but still retain some shape. Season and stir in
the parsley.

4 Toss the tomato sauce into the pasta and serve sprinkled
with the Parmesan cheese.

Tip... The sauce will be quite chunky, so if you prefer it
smoother, simply cook it for 2–3 minutes longer and then
mash or blend in a liquidiser.

Chilli and bacon pasta

Serves 4
499 calories per serving
Takes 15 minutes
❄ (for up to 1 month)

450 g (1 lb) dried tagliatelle
calorie controlled cooking spray
2 red chillies, de-seeded and chopped finely
8 rashers rindless smoked lean back bacon, chopped
325 g (11½ oz) virtually fat free fromage frais
2 tablespoons fresh shredded basil
salt and freshly ground black pepper

A fiery pasta dish that takes just 15 minutes. Serve with a large salad.

1 Bring a large pan of water to the boil and cook the pasta according to the packet instructions, until al dente.

2 Spray a frying pan with the cooking spray and heat. Add the chillies and bacon and cook for 5–6 minutes or until the bacon is crispy.

3 Drain the pasta and return to the pan with the chilli, bacon, fromage frais, basil and seasoning. Toss together and serve immediately.

Pasta arrabbiata

Serves 4
390 calories per serving
Takes 35 minutes
Ⓥ
❄ (sauce only)

calorie controlled cooking spray
1 onion, chopped finely
1 garlic clove, crushed
400 g can chopped tomatoes
2 teaspoons dried chilli flakes
½ vegetable stock cube, crumbled
1 tablespoon tomato purée
400 g (14 oz) dried fusilli pasta

This spicy tomato sauce is easy to prepare and also goes well with grilled chicken or fish.

1 Lightly coat a lidded saucepan with the cooking spray and heat until hot. Add the onion and garlic and cook for 5 minutes until beginning to brown.

2 Add the tomatoes, chilli and stock cube with 100 ml (3½ fl oz) water. Cover and simmer for 10 minutes. Stir in the tomato purée.

3 Meanwhile bring a large pan of water to the boil and cook the pasta according to the packet instructions. Drain the pasta well, add the sauce to the pan and toss to mix.

Tip… Make a double quantity of this sauce and freeze half for later.

Spicy sausage pasta

Serves 4
262 calories per serving
Takes 30 minutes
❄

150 g (5½ oz) dried conchiglie (pasta shells)

calorie controlled cooking spray

2 onions, sliced

175 g (6 oz) chorizo sausage, sliced thinly

1 red chilli, de-seeded and chopped finely

2 garlic cloves, crushed

1 red pepper, de-seeded and chopped

1 green pepper, de-seeded and chopped

300 g (10½ oz) chestnut mushrooms, sliced

1 teaspoon dried basil

6 fresh plum tomatoes, skinned and chopped (see Tip)

salt and freshly ground black pepper

Chorizo is intensely flavoured, which means a little goes a long way in this fresh tomato sauce.

1 Bring a large pan of water to the boil and cook the pasta according to the packet instructions. When ready, drain and keep warm.

2 Meanwhile, heat a large lidded pan, spray with the cooking spray and gently fry the onions for 2 minutes. Turn up the heat and add the sausage, chilli, garlic and peppers and continue to fry for 3 minutes more. Add the mushrooms and basil, mix well and fry for a further 3 minutes. Add the tomatoes and cover and simmer for 10 minutes.

3 Add the cooked pasta to the pan, season and mix thoroughly. Bring back to a simmer and serve immediately.

Tip… To skin tomatoes, lightly score them around their middle, place in a heatproof jug or bowl and cover them with boiling water. Leave to stand for 2 minutes, then drain and cover with cold water. When cool enough to handle, the skins should slide off easily.

Summer salsa spaghetti

Serves 2
262 calories per serving
Takes 20 minutes

100 g (3½ oz) dried spaghetti

2 large ripe tomatoes, chopped finely

1 red onion, chopped very finely

2 tablespoons small capers in brine, drained

40 g (1½ oz) pimiento-stuffed olives, halved

½ teaspoon finely chopped red chilli

zest and juice of ½ a lemon, to taste

3 tablespoons shredded fresh basil

salt and freshly ground black pepper

This toss-and-serve pasta dish has a no-cook dressing that is packed full of Mediterranean flavours. Make sure you use really ripe tomatoes for the best colour and taste.

1 Bring a large pan of water to the boil, snap the spaghetti in half, add to the pan and cook according to the packet instructions, until al dente.

2 Meanwhile, mix the tomatoes with the onion, capers, olives, chilli, lemon zest and basil.

3 Drain the pasta and return it to the pan. Tip the tomato mixture into the pan and toss well. Season and drizzle over the lemon juice, to taste. Serve immediately.

Variation… As a change from lemon, try balsamic vinegar. You will need about 1 teaspoon to replace the juice and zest.

Pork goulash with tagliatelle

Serves 4

527 calories per serving

Takes 30 minutes to prepare,
20 minutes to cook

❄ (goulash only)

calorie controlled cooking
    spray
450 g (1 lb) onions, chopped
2 garlic cloves, crushed
**2 red peppers, de-seeded and
    chopped**
**400 g (14 oz) lean pork steaks,
    fat removed, and cut in bite
    size pieces**
**200 g (7 oz) mushrooms,
    halved**
600 ml (20 fl oz) tomato juice
½ teaspoon paprika
**a few thyme or rosemary
    sprigs, tough stems
    removed, leaves chopped**
350 g (12 oz) dried tagliatelle
**salt and freshly ground black
    pepper**

*A substantial warming dish with a hint of spice for all
the family to enjoy.*

1 Heat a large lidded non-stick saucepan or flameproof
casserole dish and spray with the cooking spray. Add the
onions, garlic and peppers. Cook for 15 minutes, stirring
occasionally, or until the vegetables are softened, adding
a little water if necessary to prevent them from sticking.

2 Meanwhile, heat a large non-stick frying pan and spray
with cooking spray. Season the pork and fry over a high heat
until browned all over. Add the mushrooms and stir-fry for
a further 2–4 minutes.

3 Add the pork and mushrooms to the casserole or saucepan,
together with the tomato juice, paprika and herbs. Bring to the
boil and then simmer, covered, for 20 minutes, until the sauce
is reduced and the pork is tender.

4 After 5 minutes, bring a large pan of water to the boil and
cook the pasta according to the packet instructions, until
tender. Drain and serve topped with the goulash.

Grilled teriyaki salmon and pasta

Serves 1
411 calories per serving
Takes 20 minutes +
marinating

100 g (3½ oz) salmon fillet
**2 tablespoons teriyaki
marinade**
**40 g (1½ oz) dried quick cook
spaghetti**
**60 g (2 oz) long stemmed
broccoli or broccoli florets**
2 tomatoes, halved
**1 tablespoon chopped fresh
coriander leaves**
**finely grated zest and juice of
½ a lime**

*Teriyaki is a Japanese marinade made from soy sauce,
wine, garlic and spices. It's great for flavouring fish,
chicken and vegetables.*

1 Place the salmon in a non-metallic bowl. Pour over
1 tablespoon of the teriyaki marinade, cover and leave to
marinate for at least 10 minutes.

2 Bring a large pan of water to the boil and cook the pasta
according to the packet instructions. Add the broccoli for the
final 4 minutes of cooking time. Drain and rinse thoroughly.

3 Preheat the grill to medium and line the grill pan with foil.
Brush the tomatoes with the remaining teriyaki marinade and
place on the grill pan with the salmon. Grill for 8 minutes,
turning halfway through, until the salmon just flakes.

4 Mix the coriander leaves, lime zest and juice into the pasta
and broccoli mixture and serve topped with the salmon and
tomatoes.

Tips… Try to marinate the salmon for at least 30 minutes
to get the maximum flavour. You could prepare it before
you go to work, then cover and refrigerate it until you're
ready to cook.

For an extra kick, try garnishing with half a finely cubed
red chilli.

Spaghetti amatriciana

Serves 1
342 calories per serving
Takes 40 minutes

❄ (sauce only)

2 vegetarian bacon rashers,
  chopped roughly
calorie controlled cooking
  spray
½ onion, chopped
1 large garlic clove, chopped
125 g (4½ oz) passata
1 teaspoon tomato ketchup
a large pinch of dried chilli
  flakes
30 g (1¼ oz) frozen petits pois
60 g (2 oz) dried wholemeal
  spaghetti
salt and freshly ground black
  pepper

This vegetarian version of the classic Italian pasta dish features meat-free bacon rashers in a tomato and pea sauce. Serve with broccoli florets.

1 Heat a lidded non-stick saucepan. Spray the bacon with the cooking spray, and cook for 3–4 minutes until starting to colour. Add the onion to the pan, spray again with cooking spray and cook, covered and stirring occasionally, for 8 minutes until softened. Add the garlic and cook for another minute.

2 Add the passata and ketchup to the pan, bring to the boil, reduce the heat to low and simmer, partially covered, for 8–10 minutes until reduced and thickened. Stir in the chilli flakes and petits pois, and cook for a minute or so until tender.

3 Meanwhile, bring a large pan of water to the boil and cook the pasta according to the packet instructions. Drain, reserving 2 tablespoons of the cooking water.

4 Stir the pasta, reserved cooking water and bacon into the tomato sauce and turn until coated. Season then serve immediately.

Turkey salsa tagliatelle

Serves 2
472 calories per serving
Takes 20 minutes

150 g (5½ oz) dried tagliatelle
calorie controlled cooking
  spray
250 g (9 oz) lean turkey
  breast steaks, cut into bite
  size strips
½ onion, chopped finely
1 garlic clove, crushed
25 g (1 oz) jalapeño peppers in
  brine, drained and chopped
5 ripe tomatoes, de-seeded
  and cubed
½ x 25 g packet fresh
  coriander, leaves chopped
salt and freshly ground black
  pepper

This light, fresh tomato sauce is perfect for pasta but be warned, it is hot and fiery. To turn down the heat, either use fewer jalapeño peppers or use 1 large, de-seeded and cubed green pepper instead.

1 Bring a pan of water to the boil and cook the tagliatelle according to packet instructions, until al dente.

2 Meanwhile, heat a non-stick frying pan until hot and spray with the cooking spray. Add the turkey strips and cook for 3 minutes until brown all over. Then add the onion and cook for 3 minutes. Stir in the garlic, jalapeño peppers and half the tomatoes. Gently cook for 3 minutes until warmed through and the turkey is cooked.

3 Drain the pasta, reserving a ladleful of cooking liquid in the pan. Return the pasta to the pan. Stir through the turkey mixture, remaining tomatoes and coriander. Check the seasoning and serve immediately.

Variation… Replace the turkey with 175 g (6 oz) Quorn Chicken Style Pieces or simply omit the turkey and add two more tomatoes for a simple sauce.

Persian turkey pasta

Serves 4

565 calories per serving

Takes 25 minutes +
10 minutes – 8 hours
marinating

**350 g (12 oz) turkey stir-fry
strips**

**450 g (1 lb) low fat natural
yogurt**

2 teaspoons ground cumin

1 teaspoon cinnamon

1 teaspoon cayenne pepper

**150 g (5½ oz) dried apricots,
chopped**

350 g (12 oz) pasta shapes

25 g (1 oz) flaked almonds

juice of ½ a lemon

**chopped fresh mint, to serve
(optional)**

**salt and freshly ground black
pepper**

*Strips of turkey are baked with low fat natural yogurt,
spices and apricots and a sprinkling of toasted almonds
for a delicious, light supper dish.*

1 In a bowl mix the turkey strips with the yogurt, spices,
apricots and seasoning. Leave in the fridge for as long as
possible (at least 10 minutes, ideally overnight).

2 Preheat the oven to Gas Mark 9/240°C/fan oven 220°C.

3 Bring a saucepan of water to the boil and cook the pasta
according to the packet instructions. Drain and keep warm.

4 Place the turkey and the marinade on a deep baking tray
and bake for 15 minutes. Remove from the oven and pour
off any juices in the tray. Reserve the juices.

5 Heat the grill and toast the flaked almonds.

6 In a large bowl toss together the turkey, its juices, the
almonds and pasta. Add some seasoning and lemon juice
to taste. Sprinkle with chopped mint, if using, and serve.

Something special

Pasta in a paper bag

Serves 4
248 calories per serving
Takes 40 minutes

calorie controlled cooking
  spray
2 garlic cloves, sliced
2 rashers smoked lean back
  bacon, cut into strips
450 g (1 lb) baby plum
  tomatoes, halved
290 g jar roasted peppers in
  vinegar, drained and sliced
4 fresh rosemary sprigs
150 ml (5 fl oz) dry white wine
4 tablespoons vegetable stock
175 g (6 oz) dried spaghetti,
  broken into approximately
  6 cm (2½ inch) pieces
10 stoned black olives in
  brine, halved
salt and freshly ground black
  pepper
4 lemon wedges, to serve

A nice trick for a dinner party: the pasta finishes cooking in its own parchment parcel.

1 Preheat the oven to Gas Mark 6/200°C/fan oven 180°C. Spray a lidded, non-stick frying pan with the cooking spray. Heat until sizzling then add the garlic and bacon and stir-fry for 3 minutes until golden. Remove from the pan. Set aside.

2 Spray the pan again, add the tomatoes, peppers and rosemary and cook for 2 minutes. Add the white wine and stock, bring to the boil, cover and simmer for 5 minutes until soft. Season.

3 Cut 4 baking parchment 40 cm (16 inch) squares and place them on two baking trays. Bring a large pan of water to the boil and cook the pasta for half the cooking time stated in the packet instructions. Drain thoroughly and mix with the tomato sauce.

4 Divide the mixture between the four pieces of parchment, top with the bacon and garlic mix and the olives. Scrunch up the paper to form a parcel. Bake in the oven for 8 minutes or until the pasta is just cooked – open one of the parcels to check, but beware of the hot steam. Serve each parcel on a plate and let guests open their own. Serve each with a lemon wedge, to garnish.

Butternut squash and goat's cheese penne

Serves 1
315 calories per serving
Takes 25 minutes

50 g (1¾ oz) dried penne pasta
calorie controlled cooking
 spray
150 g (5½ oz) butternut
 squash, de-seeded and
 chopped into bite size pieces
1 garlic clove, sliced
3 fresh sage leaves, shredded
salt and freshly ground black
 pepper
25 g (1 oz) soft goat's cheese,
 crumbled or cut into small
 pieces, to serve

*The sweetness of the butternut squash complements the
tangy goat's cheese and sage.*

1 Bring a pan of water to the boil and cook the pasta according
to the packet instructions. Drain, reserving 2 tablespoons of
cooking liquid, and set aside.

2 Lightly coat a medium non-stick frying pan with the cooking
spray and heat until hot. Add the butternut squash and stir-fry
for 5 minutes or until tender. Add the garlic and sage and cook
for a further minute.

3 Add the pasta and reserved cooking liquid, and stir through
until hot. Remove from the heat, season and serve with the
goat's cheese on top.

Tip… If you prefer, use 25 g (1 oz) grated reduced fat
Cheddar cheese, sprinkled over the top.

Baked aubergine pasta

Serves 4
365 calories per serving
Takes 45 minutes

2 aubergines
4 garlic cloves, unpeeled
350 g (12 oz) dried pasta
4 tablespoons half fat crème fraîche
juice of ½ a lemon
25 g packet fresh basil or parsley, chopped
salt and freshly ground black pepper

In this recipe aubergines are baked slowly and then mixed with half fat crème fraîche and garlic to make a wonderful pasta sauce.

1 Preheat the oven to Gas Mark 6/200°C/fan oven 180°C. Place the aubergines and the garlic on a roasting tray and bake for 40 minutes, turning once.

2 Meanwhile, bring a large pan of water to the boil and cook the pasta according to the packet instructions. Drain.

3 When the aubergines are cooked, cut them in half lengthways and spoon out the soft flesh into a bowl. Pop the garlic out of its skin and add to the aubergine. Add the crème fraîche, lemon juice and seasoning and mash everything together.

4 Return the pasta to the pan and stir in the sauce over a low heat to warm it through, then sprinkle with fresh basil or parsley.

Pasta cocktail

Serves 6
105 calories per serving
Takes 20 minutes

75 g (2¾ oz) dried pasta shapes

4 tablespoons extra light mayonnaise

2 tablespoons tomato ketchup

2 tablespoons low fat natural yogurt

2 teaspoons lemon juice

a dash of Tabasco sauce

3 celery sticks, chopped

1 red or yellow pepper, de-seeded and chopped

10 cm (4 inches) cucumber, chopped

1 red apple, cored and chopped

a few crisp lettuce leaves, shredded

salt and freshly ground black pepper

lemon wedges, to garnish

This refreshing dinner-party starter combines crunchy vegetables with crisp apple in a delicious dressing.

1 Bring a large pan of water to the boil and cook the pasta according to packet instructions. Drain well and rinse with cold water to cool.

2 In a large bowl, mix together the mayonnaise, tomato sauce, yogurt, lemon juice and Tabasco.

3 Tip the pasta into the sauce and add the celery, pepper, cucumber and apple. Season lightly, then mix together gently.

4 Line six individual serving dishes with shredded lettuce, then top with the pasta mixture. Garnish with lemon wedges and serve.

Tip… Add a tablespoon of chopped fresh herbs to the mixture; mint, chives or parsley all taste delicious in this recipe.

Variation… Vary the vegetables according to your personal preferences. Radishes, tomatoes, cucumber and red onion make a tasty combination.

Lamb, spinach and pasta soup

Serves 2
447 calories per serving
Takes 40 minutes
❄

200 g (7 oz) lean lamb steaks,
visible fat removed, cut into
large bite size pieces
calorie controlled cooking
spray
1 onion, chopped
1 carrot, peeled and sliced
1 celery stick, sliced
300 ml (10 fl oz) hot vegetable
stock
200 ml (7 fl oz) passata
1 fresh rosemary sprig
½ teaspoon harissa paste
1 teaspoon tomato purée
75 g (2¾ oz) spinach leaves or
green cabbage, shredded
100 g (3½ oz) dried
wholewheat farfalle
salt and freshly ground black
pepper
a handful of fresh basil leaves,
to garnish

*Hearty and filling, this is just the thing for a warming and
cosy supper for two.*

1 Heat a large, lidded, non-stick saucepan until hot. Spray the
lamb with the cooking spray then cook for 3 minutes, turning
once, until browned all over. Remove from the pan and cover
with foil.

2 Add the onion, carrot and celery to the pan and spray with
the cooking spray. Cook, stirring occasionally, over a medium
heat for 2 minutes.

3 Pour in the stock and passata, add the rosemary sprig, and
bring to the boil. Reduce the heat, stir in the harissa paste,
tomato purée and lamb then simmer, partially covered, for
15 minutes to reduce the liquid. Add the spinach or cabbage,
season and cook for another 3 minutes until tender.

4 Meanwhile, bring a large pan of water to the boil and cook
the pasta according to the packet instructions, until al dente.
Drain the pasta and add to the pan. Season and sprinkle with
the basil leaves. Remove the rosemary sprig before serving.

Ⓥ **Variation…** Swap the lamb for 200 g (7 oz) canned chick
peas. Add them with the harissa paste in step 3.

Mixed mushroom pasta

Serves 4

575 calories per serving

Takes 20 minutes to prepare,
20 minutes to cook

250 g (9 oz) dried pasta

2 tablespoons olive oil

2 garlic cloves, chopped

110 g (4 oz) baby button
mushrooms

175 g (6 oz) chestnut
mushrooms, quartered

175 g (6 oz) small open-cup
mushrooms, sliced

1 teaspoon dried rosemary

2 tablespoons plain flour

150 ml (5 fl oz) skimmed milk

350 g (12 oz) virtually fat free
fromage frais

60 g (2 oz) Cheddar cheese,
grated

salt and freshly ground black
pepper

fresh parsley, chopped, to
serve

Using a mixture of mushrooms adds depth of flavour to this creamy pasta bake. Serve it with a crisp salad.

1 Preheat the oven to Gas Mark 5/190°C/fan oven 170°C.

2 Bring a large pan of water to the boil and cook the pasta according to the packet instructions. Drain well.

3 Meanwhile, heat the oil in a large frying pan then fry the garlic, mushrooms and rosemary for 10 minutes over a low heat. Season to taste.

4 Stir in the flour and cook for 1 minute. Then gradually add the milk, stirring continuously, until thickened.

5 Remove the pan from the heat and transfer the mushroom mixture to a large ovenproof dish. Stir in the drained pasta, the fromage frais and seasoning.

6 Sprinkle the Cheddar cheese over the dish, then bake for 20 minutes or until bubbling. Serve immediately, garnished with a sprinkling of parsley.

Tip… Use calorie controlled cooking spray instead of olive oil to save on calories.

Slow cooked beef and pasta casserole

Serves 6

385 calories per serving

Takes 20 minutes to prepare,
1¾ hours to cook

❄ (beef casserole without the
pasta)

calorie controlled cooking
spray

750 g (1 lb 10 oz) lean beef
casserole steak, cubed

1 large onion, sliced

3 lean back bacon rashers,
chopped

4 garlic cloves, crushed

700 g jar passata with basil

18 stoned black olives in
brine, drained

600 ml (20 fl oz) hot beef
stock

300 g (10½ oz) mushrooms,
chopped roughly

225 g (8 oz) dried fusilli or
penne

salt and freshly ground black
pepper

*A richly flavoured and filling all-in-one casserole, ideal for
a special family weekend meal.*

1 Preheat the oven to Gas Mark 1/140°C/fan oven 120°C.
Heat a large, non-stick frying pan until hot and spray with the
cooking spray. Season the beef, brown it in two batches, then
remove to a plate.

2 Meanwhile, heat a lidded, flameproof casserole on the hob
and spray with the cooking spray. Add the onion and cook for
3–4 minutes. Add the bacon and garlic and cook for 2 minutes,
then stir in the beef, passata and olives.

3 Use a little of the stock to deglaze the frying pan, stirring,
then pour this liquid and the rest of the stock in to the casserole.
Bring to a simmer, cover and transfer to the oven for 1¼ hours.

4 Stir in the mushrooms and cook for a further 15 minutes.

5 Finally, add the pasta, pushing it into the sauce. Cover and
cook in the oven for 15–20 minutes, or until the beef is tender
and the pasta is cooked.

Roasted sausage and pepper rigatoni

Serves 4

433 calories per serving

Takes 10 minutes to prepare,
30 minutes to cook

454 g packet low fat sausages

1 red pepper, de-seeded and chopped roughly

1 yellow pepper, de-seeded and chopped roughly

3 garlic cloves, crushed

a pinch of dried chillies

calorie controlled cooking spray

350 g (12 oz) cherry tomatoes, halved

250 g (9 oz) dried rigatoni

2 heaped tablespoons shredded fresh basil

Here is a deliciously different take on pasta, with a roasted vegetable and sausage sauce. Great for when you've got friends over midweek.

1 Preheat the oven to Gas Mark 7/220°C/fan oven 200°C. Snip the sausages into chunks using kitchen scissors and toss together with the peppers, garlic and chillies in a large roasting tin. Spray with the cooking spray and roast for 15 minutes.

2 Stir the cherry tomatoes into the roasting tin and cook for a further 10–15 minutes.

3 Meanwhile, bring a large pan of water to the boil and cook the pasta according to the packet instructions. Drain thoroughly.

4 Add the pasta to the roasted sausage and pepper mixture and stir in the fresh basil. Serve immediately.

❂ **Variation…** Use Quorn Cumberland sausages instead of pork sausages.

Pasta with feta and mint

Serves 2
356 calories per serving
Takes 25 minutes

125 g (4½ oz) dried linguine
1 courgette, grated
1 leek, sliced thinly
75 g (2¾ oz) frozen petits pois
calorie controlled cooking
  spray
1 teaspoon olive oil
2 garlic cloves, crushed
1 tablespoon lemon juice
4 tablespoons chopped fresh
  mint
75 g (2¾ oz) light feta cheese,
  cubed
salt and freshly ground black
  pepper

*A delightfully summery pasta dish to share on a warm
summer evening.*

1 Bring a large pan of water to the boil and cook the pasta
according to the packet instructions, adding the courgette, leek
and peas for the last minute of cooking time. Drain the pasta
and vegetables, reserving 6 tablespoons of the cooking liquid.

2 Heat a large non-stick frying pan, spray with the cooking
spray, add the olive oil and garlic and cook for 1 minute until
softened. Add the pasta, vegetables and reserved cooking
water then stir until warmed through.

3 Remove from the heat and stir in the lemon juice, mint and
feta cheese. Season, toss until combined and then serve.

Variation… Instead of the feta, add 250 g (9 oz) skinless,
boneless chicken breasts, cut into bite size pieces. Cook
in a non-stick frying pan sprayed with cooking spray,
for 6–8 minutes until golden and cooked through, then
continue with the recipe in step 2.

Roasted cod and butternut squash linguine

Serves 1

611 calories per serving

Takes 20 minutes to prepare,
35 minutes to cook

**½ small butternut squash,
de-seeded and cut into small
cubes**

**1 small red onion, cut into thin
wedges**

1 fresh rosemary sprig

1 fresh thyme sprig

**calorie controlled cooking
spray**

200 g (7 oz) skinless cod fillet

40 g (1½ oz) dried linguine

**2 tablespoons fat free
dressing**

**salt and freshly ground black
pepper**

*A sophisticated supper for one that's a great way to cook
cod and just right for when you fancy a treat.*

1 Preheat the oven to Gas Mark 7/220°C/fan oven 200°C.
Place the squash, onion and herbs in a large roasting tin.
Spray with the cooking spray and roast for 20 minutes,
stirring occasionally.

2 Season the cod and sit it on top of the squash and onion.
Roast for a further 15 minutes until the vegetables are lightly
charred and the cod flakes with a fork. Once cooked, flake the
fish into chunks.

3 Meanwhile, bring a large pan of water to the boil and
cook the pasta according to the packet instructions. Drain
well and rinse.

4 Mix the dressing into the pasta, then add the vegetables
and the cod, along with any caramelised bits from the tin.
Mix together well and serve.

Variation... Use two chopped carrots instead of the
butternut squash.

Spaghetti with green beans, peas and ham

Serves 4
340 calories per serving
Takes 15 minutes

225 g (8 oz) dried spaghetti
2 teaspoons low fat spread
1 small onion, finely chopped
100 g (3½ oz) fine green beans, trimmed and chopped
100 g (3½ oz) lean cooked ham, chopped
75 g (2¾ oz) frozen petits pois or garden peas
225 g (8 oz) virtually fat free fromage frais
100 g (3½ oz) low fat soft cheese with garlic and herbs
a few basil leaves, torn into shreds, plus whole leaves to garnish
salt and freshly ground black pepper

A quick creamy sauce for spaghetti that will impress friends who drop by for dinner.

1 Bring a large pan of water to the boil and cook the spaghetti according to packet instructions.

2 Meanwhile, heat the low fat spread in a saucepan and sauté the onion until softened, about 3 minutes. Add the green beans, ham and frozen peas. Cook, stirring, for 2–3 minutes. Add the fromage frais, soft cheese and basil leaves to the saucepan. Heat gently, stirring from time to time, for about 4 minutes. Season with salt and black pepper.

3 Drain the spaghetti well and return to the pan. Add the sauce and stir gently to mix. Transfer to four warmed plates and serve at once, garnished with the basil leaves.

Tip… Any pasta shapes will work well with this sauce.

Seafood tagliatelle

Serves 2
366 calories per serving
Takes 25 minutes

calorie controlled cooking
  spray
1 red onion, chopped
400 g can chopped tomatoes
  with garlic and herbs
½ teaspoon chilli powder
110 g (4 oz) dried tagliatelle
250 g packet mixed seafood
  such as prawns, mussels,
  squid
2 teaspoons half fat crème
  fraîche
2 tablespoons finely chopped
  fresh parsley, to garnish

Take advantage of supermarket packets of ready-mixed seafood for this quick supper for two – it's a great Friday night treat after a busy week.

1 Spray a frying pan with the cooking spray and heat until hot. Add the onion and stir-fry for 5 minutes until tender. Add the tomatoes and chilli powder, reduce the heat and let the sauce simmer for 10 minutes.

2 Meanwhile, bring a large pan of water to the boil and cook the pasta according to the packet instructions. Drain and return to the pan.

3 Add the seafood and tomato sauce to the pasta, with the crème fraîche, and heat for 2–3 minutes until hot. Serve in bowls garnished with parsley.

Roast vegetable lasagne

Serves 6

300 calories per serving

Takes 30 minutes to prepare,
30 minutes to cook

1 courgette

1 large carrot

1 red and 1 yellow pepper

1 leek, sliced

6 tomatoes, quartered

1 garlic clove, chopped

2 teaspoons sesame oil

455 g jar reduced fat tomato
pasta sauce

9 sheets lasagne verdi

150 g (5½ oz) half fat Cheddar
cheese, grated

salt and freshly ground black
pepper

For the béchamel sauce

600 ml (20 fl oz) skimmed milk

½ a carrot

½ an onion

8 peppercorns and 4 cloves

1 teaspoon ground mace

1 bay leaf

30 g (1¼ oz) plain flour

2 teaspoons low fat spread

A fantastic low calorie vegetarian version of lasagne.
Serve it with your favourite salad for easy entertaining.

1 Preheat the oven to Gas Mark 6/ 200°C/fan oven 180°C.
Cut the courgette and carrot into chunks and de-seed and slice
the peppers. Slice the leek and quarter the tomatoes. Place all
the vegetables and garlic in a roasting dish. Season, sprinkle
with sesame oil and toss them together. Roast for 30 minutes
until the vegetables are tender and crispy around the edges.

2 Meanwhile make the béchamel sauce. Heat the milk in a
saucepan with the carrot, onion, peppercorns, cloves, mace
and bay leaf. Bring to the boil, then turn off the heat. Leave
for 15 minutes before straining.

3 In a medium saucepan whisk together the flour, low fat
spread and a few tablespoons of the infused milk to make a
paste. Add the rest of the milk and place on the hob. Bring to
the boil, whisking continuously. Turn down the heat. Simmer
for 5 minutes until smooth and thick. Season.

4 Combine the roasted vegetables with the tomato pasta
sauce. Use a third of the vegetable mixture to cover the bottom
of a 30 x 23 cm (12 x 9 inch) ovenproof dish. Top the mixture
with three sheets of lasagne, just under a third of the sauce
and a handful of grated cheese. Repeat the layers twice, ending
with just over a third of the sauce, and the remaining cheese.

5 Bake in the oven for 25–30 minutes, until cooked through
and golden.

Tip... Make sure you buy vegetarian half fat Cheddar.

Smoked ham pasta with olives and lemon

Serves 4
335 calories per serving
Takes 15 minutes

**300 g (10½ oz) dried
tagliatelle**
75 g (2¾ oz) mange tout
**16 cherry tomatoes on the
vine, halved**
**150 g (5½ oz) wafer thin
smoked ham, cut into strips**
**60 g (2 oz) stoned black olives
in brine, drained and halved**
zest and juice of a lemon
**salt and freshly ground black
pepper**
lemon wedges, to serve

*This makes a tasty yet simple midweek supper and is
delicious with a green salad.*

1 Bring a large pan of water to the boil and cook the pasta
according to the packet instructions. Add the mange tout for
the last minute of cooking time. Drain, reserving 4 tablespoons
of the cooking liquid and return the pasta, mange tout and
reserved liquid to the pan.

2 Add the remaining ingredients and mix well. Leave on a low
heat for 1–2 minutes until everything is hot. Season and serve
immediately with lemon wedges to squeeze over.

Variations… Using the zest and juice of a lime also works
well in this dish.

A generous handful of rocket or watercress makes a good
addition – just toss it in at the last minute.

Replace the ham with 125 g (4½ oz) smoked salmon
trimmings for a change.

Spaghetti with smoked salmon and dill

Serves 2
313 calories per serving
Takes 15 minutes

125 g (4½ oz) dried spaghetti

60 g (2 oz) runner beans, cut into 2 cm (¾ inch) pieces

60 g (2 oz) smoked salmon, cut into 3 cm (1¼ inch) strips

150 g (5½ oz) virtually fat free fromage frais

1 tablespoon roughly chopped fresh dill or 1 teaspoon dried dill

finely grated zest of ½ a lemon, plus wedges, to serve

freshly ground black pepper

Smoked salmon in a creamy dill and lemon sauce makes a really quick and easy yet special meal for two.

1 Bring a large pan of water to the boil and cook the pasta according to the packet instructions, adding the beans for the last 5 minutes of cooking time. Reserve 2 tablespoons of cooking liquid. Drain the pasta and beans and rinse thoroughly, then return them to the pan.

2 Add the smoked salmon, fromage frais, half the dill, lemon zest and reserved cooking liquid to the pasta mixture. Stir to mix over a medium heat, for 1 minute until hot – no longer, to prevent the sauce curdling. Divide between two plates and sprinkle with the remaining dill. Serve with a lemon wedge each and season with black pepper.

Variation... Try adding 60 g (2 oz) cooked, peeled prawns for an extra treat. Add them after step 1 and heat for 2 minutes.

Spinach and mushroom cannelloni

Serves 4
359 calories per serving
Takes 45 minutes

calorie controlled cooking spray
300 g (10½ oz) mushrooms, chopped finely
2 garlic cloves, crushed
450 g (1 lb) spinach leaves
4 tablespoons tomato purée
2 teaspoons dried thyme
16 dried cannelloni tubes (about 150 g/5½ oz)
600 ml (20 fl oz) skimmed milk
3 tablespoons cornflour
1 tablespoon wholegrain mustard
75 g (2¾ oz) half fat Cheddar cheese, grated
25 g (1 oz) Parmesan cheese, grated
2 tomatoes, sliced
salt and freshly ground black pepper
crisp green salad leaves, sliced red onion and cucumber, to serve

A perfect dish for a dinner party – whether your guests are vegetarian or not, it's sure to be popular.

1 Preheat the oven to Gas Mark 6/200°C/fan oven 180°C. Spray a large pan with the cooking spray and when it is hot, add the mushrooms and cook over a medium heat for 3 minutes until the juices begin to flow. Add the garlic and continue cooking for 2 minutes until the juices have evaporated.

2 Add the spinach in batches and cook, stirring until wilted. Remove from the heat and stir in the tomato purée, thyme and seasoning. Leave to cool slightly.

3 Using the end of a teaspoon, stuff the cannelloni tubes with the spinach and mushroom mixture and place in a single layer in a baking dish.

4 Reserving 4 tablespoons of milk, bring the rest to the boil in a saucepan. Blend the cornflour with the reserved milk to make a paste and stir into the pan. While stirring, bring the sauce back to the boil and cook until thickened. It should still be quite runny. Remove the sauce from the heat. Add the mustard and half of each of the Cheddar and Parmesan cheeses. Season.

5 Pour the sauce over the cannelloni, top with the tomato slices and sprinkle with the remaining cheeses. Bake for 30 minutes until golden. Serve four tubes each with the salad leaves, red onion and cucumber.

Penne with lamb ragù

Serves 6

376 calories per serving

Takes 15 minutes to prepare,
  45 minutes to cook

❄ (ragù sauce only)

calorie controlled cooking
  spray
**500 g (1 lb 2 oz) lean lamb
  mince**
2 onions, chopped finely
3 garlic cloves, crushed
2 teaspoons dried mint
½ teaspoon ground cinnamon
**2 x 400 g cans chopped
  tomatoes**
350 g (12 oz) dried penne
salt and freshly ground black
  pepper

*A twist on spaghetti Bolognese, this lamb version is
seasoned with a touch of mint and cinnamon, giving it
a hint of Greek flavouring.*

1 Heat a lidded, flameproof casserole dish on the hob and
spray with the cooking spray. Add the lamb mince and the
onions and cook for 5 minutes, stirring frequently to break
up the mince.

2 Add the garlic, mint and cinnamon to the casserole and cook
for 1 minute before stirring in the tomatoes and seasoning.
Bring to a simmer, cover and cook gently for 45 minutes.

3 Around 20 minutes before the sauce is ready, bring a large
pan of water to the boil and cook the pasta according to the
packet instructions. Drain and toss with the ragù sauce. Serve
immediately.

Ⓥ **Variation…** Replace the lamb mince with Quorn mince.
Quorn doesn't need to be browned so add it in step 2 with
the garlic, mint and cinnamon.

Turkey and broccoli pasta with mustard crème fraîche

Serves 4
305 calories per serving
Takes 25 minutes

175 g (6 oz) dried pasta
275 g (9½ oz) broccoli florets
275 g (9½ oz) turkey breast strips
1 small onion, chopped
125 g (4½ oz) mushrooms, sliced
200 ml (7 fl oz) hot chicken stock
2 teaspoons cornflour
4 tablespoons half fat crème fraîche
1 tablespoon Dijon mustard
freshly ground black pepper

Crème fraîche and mustard make a sophisticated sauce for this easy supper for four.

1 Bring a large pan of water to the boil and cook the pasta according to the packet instructions. Add the broccoli to the pan halfway through the cooking time.

2 Meanwhile, dry-fry the turkey, onion and mushrooms for 3–4 minutes in a large non-stick frying pan. Pour in the hot stock and bring to the boil. Blend the cornflour with the crème fraîche and stir in the mustard. Stir the mixture into the pan. Simmer for 5 minutes.

3 Thoroughly drain the pasta and broccoli. Combine them with the turkey and sauce. Season well, with plenty of black pepper, divide between warmed bowls and serve.

Variation... Add a teaspoon of garlic purée to the turkey at stage 2.

Tortelloni and vegetables en brodo

Serves 2
260 calories per serving
Takes 30 minutes

calorie controlled cooking spray
1 small onion, sliced
1 carrot, sliced thinly diagonally
3 runner beans, sliced thinly diagonally
600 ml (20 fl oz) vegetable stock
1 courgette, sliced thinly diagonally
110 g (4 oz) spring greens, shredded
225 g (8 oz) fresh tortelloni pasta filled with spinach and ricotta
15 g (½ oz) Parmesan cheese shavings
2 teaspoons low fat pesto
salt and freshly ground black pepper
a few fresh basil leaves, to garnish

This stuffed pasta soup makes a light and summery supper dish or lunch.

1 Heat a large, lidded, non-stick saucepan. Spray with the cooking spray and cook the onion, covered, for 5 minutes, stirring occasionally. Add the carrot and runner beans and cook for another 2 minutes, stirring regularly.

2 Add the stock, bring to the boil then reduce the heat and simmer for about 6 minutes, partially covered, until the vegetables are almost tender. Add the courgette and spring greens and cook for a further 2 minutes.

3 Meanwhile, bring a large pan of water to the boil and cook the tortelloni according to the packet instructions. Drain and divide between two large shallow bowls.

4 Using a slotted spoon, scoop out the cooked vegetables and divide between the bowls. Pour the stock over and season to taste. Sprinkle with the Parmesan cheese and top with a spoonful of the pesto and a few basil leaves.

Mushroom and sweet onion pasta

Serves 4
375 calories per serving
Takes 35 minutes

350 g (12 oz) dried pasta
   shapes
calorie controlled cooking
   spray
4 onions, sliced
250 g (9 oz) mushrooms,
   sliced
300 ml (10 fl oz) vegetable
   stock
4 tablespoons virtually fat free
   fromage frais
leaves from 4 fresh thyme
   sprigs
salt and freshly ground black
   pepper

*A lovely, mellow-flavoured pasta, perfect for an autumnal
evening meal.*

1 Bring a large pan of water to the boil and cook the pasta
according to the packet instructions.

2 Meanwhile, spray a large frying pan with the cooking spray
and put on a high heat. Stir-fry the onions and mushrooms for
5 minutes until they are golden brown, then add the stock and
simmer for 15 minutes.

3 Add 4 tablespoons of the pasta cooking liquid to the onion
mixture, then drain the pasta and add to the pan, along with the
fromage frais, thyme and seasoning. Toss and serve.

Tips… Make sure you buy fromage frais that is suitable for
vegetarians.

For a richer flavour use half fat crème fraîche instead of
the fromage frais.

Index

Other titles in the Weight Watchers Mini Series

ISBN 978-0-85720-932-0   ISBN 978-0-85720-935-1   ISBN 978-0-85720-934-4   ISBN 978-0-85720-938-2   ISBN 978-0-85720-931-3

ISBN 978-0-85720-937-5   ISBN 978-0-85720-936-8   ISBN 978-0-85720-933-7   ISBN 978-1-47111-084-9   ISBN 978-1-47111-089-4

ISBN 978-1-47111-091-7   ISBN 978-1-47111-087-0   ISBN 978-1-47111-090-0   ISBN 978-1-47111-085-6   ISBN 978-1-47111-088-7

ISBN 978-1-47111-086-3   ISBN 978-1-47113-165-3   ISBN 978-1-47113-166-0   ISBN 978-1-47113-167-7   ISBN 978-1-47113-164-6

For more details please visit www.simonandschuster.co.uk